# JOHN IRVING

# MODERN LITERATURE SERIES

GENERAL EDITOR: PHILIP WINSOR

*In the same series:*

S. Y. AGNON    *Harold Fisch*
SHERWOOD ANDERSON    *Welford Dunaway Taylor*
LEONID ANDREYEV    *Josephine M. Newcombe*
ISAAC BABEL    *W. W. Hallett*
JAMES BALDWIN    *Carolyn Wedin Sylvander*
SIMONE DE BEAUVOIR    *Robert D. Cottrell*
SAUL BELLOW    *Brigitte Scheer-Schäzler*
JORGE LUIS BORGES    *George R. McMurray*
BERTOLT BRECHT    *Willy Haas*
ANTHONY BURGESS    *Samuel Coale*
ALBERT CAMUS    *Carol Petersen*
TRUMAN CAPOTE    *Helen S. Garson*
WILLA CATHER    *Dorothy Tuck McFarland*
JOHN CHEEVER    *Samuel Coale*
COLETTE    *Robert D. Cottrell*
JOSEPH CONRAD    *Martin Tucker*
JULIO CORTÁZAR    *Evelyn Picon Garfield*
JOAN DIDION    *Katherine Usher Henderson*
JOHN DOS PASSOS    *George J. Becker*
THEODORE DREISER    *James Lundquist*
FRIEDRICH DÜRRENMATT    *Armin Arnold*
T. S. ELIOT    *Burton Raffel*
WILLIAM FAULKNER    *Joachim Seyppel*
F. SCOTT FITZGERALD    *Rose Adrienne Gallo*
FORD MADOX FORD    *Sondra J. Stang*
JOHN FOWLES    *Barry N. Olshen*
MAX FRISCH    *Carol Petersen*
ROBERT FROST    *Elaine Barry*
GABRIEL GARCÍA MÁRQUEZ    *George R. McMurray*
ELLEN GLASGOW    *Marcelle Thiébaux*
MAKSIM GORKI    *Gerhard Habermann*
GÜNTER GRASS    *Kurt Lothar Tank*
ROBERT GRAVES    *Katherine Snipes*
PETER HANDKE    *Nicholas Hern*
LILLIAN HELLMAN    *Doris V. Falk*
ERNEST HEMINGWAY    *Samuel Shaw*
HERMANN HESSE    *Franz Baumer*
CHESTER HIMES    *James Lundquist*
HUGO VON HOFMANNSTHAL    *Lowell W. Bangerter*
JOHN IRVING    *Gabriel Miller*
CHRISTOPHER ISHERWOOD    *Claude J. Summers*
SARAH ORNE JEWETT    *Josephine Donovan*
UWE JOHNSON    *Mark Boulby*
JAMES JOYCE    *Armin Arnold*
*(continued on last page of book)*

# JOHN IRVING

## Gabriel Miller

**FREDERICK UNGAR PUBLISHING CO.**
NEW YORK

*for*
*Lisabeth Jane*

Copyright © 1982 by Frederick Ungar Publishing Co., Inc.
*Printed in the United States of America*

**Library of Congress Cataloging in Publication Data**
Miller, Gabriel, 1948-
  John Irving.

  (Modern literature series)
  Bibliography: p.
  Includes index.
  1. Irving, John, 1942-          2. Novelists, American
--20th century--Biography.      I. Title.      II. Series.
PS3559.R68Z78              813'.54[B]              82-2793
ISBN 0-8044-2621-X                                AACR2
ISBN 0-8044-6502-9 (pbk.)

Randall Jarrell's "The Death of the Ball Turret Gunner" is reprinted by
permission of Farrar, Straus and Giroux, Inc. from *Randall Jarrell: The
Complete Poems*. Copyright 1945, 1969 by Mrs. Randall Jarrell. Copyright
renewed © 1973 by Mrs. Randall Jarrell.

# Contents

# Preface

A book on John Irving may seem to some to be a bit premature, and I suppose to some extent it is. Why write a book now on a man who has just turned forty and who clearly promises to produce many more works that will certainly test and perhaps invalidate many of the judgments made here?

Acknowledging, therefore, the possible preliminary nature of this undertaking, I can only argue for its value as such. Few writers have so vividly captured the critical and popular imagination as Irving has done. And if the notoriety and acclaim he has received are, in the nature of hero-worship, extreme, and quite likely to be tempered as time passes, they are nonetheless deserved. With only five published books, Irving has succeeded in creating a unique world and establishing a distinctive voice, and although the body of his work does tend to rework a limited range of familiar motifs, it is also marked by a readiness to experiment with form and symbolic structure. Not content to imitate a successful pattern, Irving seems to want to take on the novel and try to adapt its possibilities to his vision. This is clearly demonstrated in the contrasting styles and shapes of his two most recent works, *The World According to Garp* and *The Hotel New Hampshire*.

Yet Irving is not interested in form as an end in itself; he does not experiment merely to play or to impress, and this sets him apart from many of his contemporaries. Form is very much a part of Irving's vision. And if his world may strike some as too violent and sordid, others cannot help but note also his generosity, his expansiveness of spirit, and his insistence on the potential for achieving a productive and rewarding life. He abundantly fulfills the function of the artist—he forces us to see, but he also helps us to live with what we see.

Despite his popularity, Irving's work has not yet received any sustained serious evaluation. Book reviews (like Irving's own world) have been excessive, either in praise or in condemnation. I hope that this study—intended to open up Irving's world and elucidate his themes—will help to stimulate a more balanced discussion and evaluation of his work.

A number of people deserve thanks for their help in preparing this book. Jane Rosenman and Lois Shapiro of E. P. Dutton were generous and helpful to me in many ways. John Irving gave up an afternoon and extended some welcome hospitality to me and my family. Pat McCarney contributed her usual scrupulous job in typing the manuscript. Don Naugle, my graduate assistant, searched out book reviews and stories and labored over the bibliography.

This book owes more than I can probably afford to admit to my colleague and friend, George Bodmer, who was always willing to discuss Irving's work with me, making suggestions and forcing me to rethink my ideas. Thanks are also due Kathy, for subjecting herself to yet another manuscript and for her suggestions, which are always penetrating and right. And, finally, to Lisabeth Jane, who has given me more joy than I ever thought possible and which I undoubtedly don't deserve.

# Chronology

| | |
|---|---|
| 1942 | March 2, born in Exeter, New Hampshire. |
| 1961 | Graduates from Phillips Exeter Academy. |
| 1961–62 | Attends University of Pittsburgh. |
| 1963–64 | Attends University of Vienna. |
| 1964 | August 20, marries Shyla Leary. |
| 1965 | Graduates from the University of New Hampshire; son Colin born. |
| 1967 | Receives M.F.A. from the University of Iowa. |
| 1968 | *Setting Free the Bears* published by Random House. |
| 1969–71 | Lives in Vienna and in Putney, Vermont; works on screenplay of *Setting Free the Bears;* son Brendan born (1970). |
| 1972 | Rockefeller Foundation Grant; *The Water-Method Man* published by Random House. |
| 1972–75 | Writer-in-residence, the University of Iowa. |
| 1974 | *The 158-Pound Marriage* published by Random House. |
| 1974–75 | National Endowment for the Arts Fellowship. |
| 1975–78 | Assistant Professor of English at Mount Holyoke College. |
| 1976–77 | Guggenheim Foundation Grant. |
| 1978 | *The World According to Garp* published by E. P. Dutton. |
| 1980 | *The World According to Garp* awarded the American Book Award as the best paperback novel of 1979. |

1981    *Time* cover story, August 31; *The Hotel New Hampshire* published by E. P. Dutton.
1982    Film of *The World According to Garp*.

# CHAPTER 1

## Life and Art

The surface facts of John Irving's life can be found in his fiction, but it is a mistake to assume that his novels are, therefore, autobiographical. The details he exploits are merely that; they do not constitute the essence of his art. Commenting on the relationship between his life and his art, Irving has declared a kind of creative independence:

> I make up all the important things. I've had a very uninteresting life. I had a happy childhood. I'm grateful for how ordinary my life is because I'm not ever tempted to think that something that happened to me is important simply because it happened to me. I have no personal axes to grind; I'm free, therefore, to imagine the best possible axe to grind—and I really mean that: that's a significant freedom from the tyranny and self-importance of autobiography in fiction.[1]

John Winslow Irving was born in Exeter, New Hampshire, on March 2, 1942, the oldest of four children of Colin F. N. (his stepfather) and Frances (Winslow) Irving. His stepfather taught Russian history and served as treasurer of Phillips Exeter Acade-

my in New Hampshire (which served as the model
for the Steering School in *The World According to Garp*).
Of his own high school days there, Irving remembered:

> I was a struggling, C/B student. It gave me a sense of
> myself, gave me confidence to be able to get through
> the place, because I knew I wasn't as bright or as quick
> as most of the kids I was there with. Concentrating and
> working hard—that's how I got through. It took me
> five years to graduate.[2]

While he was at Exeter, Irving realized that he
wanted to become a writer, and the knowledge, he
recalls, caused him "suffering":

> How lonely that was! There was nothing like majoring
> in French or going to law school or medical school to
> look forward to; I had a terrible sense of how different
> I was from all my friends, and I didn't want to be
> different at all. No kid wants to be different.[3]

He also discovered his other love, wrestling:

> Surely much more important to my life than it ever was
> to Garp's was the wrestling. . . . My wrestling coach
> really got me through the place. Wrestling became
> more and more important—metaphorically, too. I was
> not a very good wrestler, but I did well: that is, I beat a
> lot of people who were much better than I was.[4]

After graduating from Exeter, Irving spent a
year (1961–62) at the University of Pittsburgh, "because it was a good place to wrestle,"[5] leaving when he
discovered he "wasn't as good a wrestler as I had to
be." From 1963 to 1964 he studied at the University
of Vienna. He remembers his time in Vienna as a

formative experience, having much the same effect on him as it would have on Garp:

> . . . Vienna was a real place for me. It was also real in the way that anything *foreign* takes on a certain visceral novelty, *just by being so new,* that we look at everything freshly. It's an act of wonder to go about the business of buying a loaf of bread. That's not simple.
>
> I'd never seen any place like Vienna. It was so new and strange—or so *old,* as it turns out, and strange —that it forced me to pay attention to every aspect of it. Nothing else had ever demanded that kind of attention from me.
>
> And it was the first place that I'd ever really felt I was *alone.* When you go to a city university like the University of Vienna, you're not part of anything: you go to classes and then you go back to your apartment. That's it. It's just a city.
>
> I loved that. It was my first sense of anonymity— which is very important.[6]

Before leaving for Vienna, Irving had taken a summer course in German at Harvard, where he met Shyla Leary, a student at Radcliffe. He married her in the summer of 1964 in Greece.

In Europe Irving affected a Bohemian life-style, traveling about on a motorcycle, meeting painters and writers, and continuing to wrestle, sparring with various Slavic opponents; these experiences are reflected in *Setting Free the Bears* and *The 158-Pound Marriage.* In Europe he also met a man with an old trained bear, which would become a central image in many of his books, and he started work on his first novel—about some cowboys who stage a crazy rodeo in New England—but he soon abandoned this project.

Returning to the United States, Irving received his B.A. degree, cum laude, in 1965 from the Univer-

sity of New Hampshire, which he had attended
briefly before going to Vienna; there he studied with
novelists Thomas Williams *(The Hair of Harold Roux)*
and John Yount *(Wolf at the Door)*. While Irving was in
college, his first son, Colin, was born. During his
undergraduate years, Irving wrote his first two stories
to be published: "A Winter Branch" appeared in
*Redbook* in 1965, and "Weary Kingdom," though
written in 1964, was not published until 1968 in *The
Boston Review*. Both stories are interesting primarily
because of their very conservative, toneless qualities,
neither demonstrating the voice that would come to
characterize Irving's writing from the publication of
*Setting Free the Bears*.

"A Winter Branch" is the story of a man in the
midst of spiritual crisis—Harvey's life has become
humdrum and his wife loves him too much. When he
discovers that someone has been taking eggs from the
refrigerator and leaving cigarettes in exchange, Harvey is at first alarmed, but then decides that he likes
the idea of mystery in his life. He becomes annoyed at
his wife, who insists on pursuing the matter, and
when she finally solves the mystery, he feels disap-
pointed. Having punctuated Harvey's musings with
descriptions of nature, which often seems to reflect
his mood but, more importantly, teases him with its
own sense of mystery, Irving concludes the story as
Harvey, in his pajamas, walks out into a snowstorm in
the middle of the night. Clearly he must learn to
recognize and appreciate this greater mystery if he is
to solve his own personal dilemma.

"Weary Kingdom" also deals with spiritual crisis.
Its protagonist, Minna Barrett, is a fifty-five-year-old
matron of the dining hall at a junior college for
women. She lives a quiet, uneventful life highlighted
by the occasional visits of students and friends who
come to share her television set, but her serenity is

suddenly disrupted when Celeste, a young woman, is hired to help her. Minna's first meeting with Celeste is significant: entering her room late at night, she finds Celeste asleep, and when she pulls back the blanket to assure herself that the woman is really sleeping, she sees that Celeste is naked:

> . . . the faint light from the desk lamp dully illuminated the long large body of Celeste in a weird sleep. The pillow rested under her shoulder blades, tipping her head back and stretching a long, graceful neck. . . . Her breasts were rigid, full and not sagging, not fallen to her armpits.

Celeste seems to represent a physical and sexual dimension missing from Minna's own life, and her subsequent escapades upset Minna and other members of the school community. When it appears that Celeste has seduced one student's boyfriend, Minna is forced to fire her, although this action is opposed by some of the workers at the dining hall, who found Celeste's youthful presence refreshing and exciting. The story ends with Minna sitting alone in her room—"The toys of her weary mind seem lost."

Both stories are precise in detail and deliberate in development; both are rather undramatic portraits of commonplace people in commonplace surroundings. The central characters are related to other Irving heroes in their self-absorption and their need for self-integration. What is missing is Irving's comic, baroque, exaggerated style. Obviously the young writer was trying in these stories to structure the traditional well-made short story; it is an attempt that Irving later totally abandoned when he discovered his own voice.

After graduating from college, Irving went on to the University of Iowa, where he studied with Vance

Bourjaily and Kurt Vonnegut. At Iowa Irving worked on *Setting Free the Bears,* which Vonnegut read in the manuscript. Meanwhile, to help support his family, Irving tended bar and sold peanuts and pennants at football games—experiences to be recounted later on *The Water-Method Man.* Receiving his M.F.A. in 1967, he then returned to New England.[7]

In 1968 Irving's first novel, *Setting Free the Bears,* was published by Random House and fared rather well critically, although it sold only 6,228 copies.[8] The money from the sales of this book allowed Irving to buy a house in Putney, Vermont, where he lived while teaching at Windham College. He then returned to Vienna for three years, working for a time with Irvin Kershner, the film director, on the movie version of *Setting Free the Bears.* There, too, his second son, Brendan, was born. The film project did not work out, and Irving returned once more to the United States, where, with the help of a Rockefeller Foundation Grant, he completed his second novel, *The Water-Method Man* (1972), also published by Random House. This book draws heavily on Irving's film experiences with Kershner, and in it, for the first time, Irving makes use of explicit details from his own life in his fiction—as he would do in his subsequent novels as well. Again, the reviews were mostly favorable, but again, the book did not sell well, its sales of 6,906 copies just slightly bettering that of the previous work.[9]

Following the publication of *The Water-Method Man,* Irving spent three years as writer-in-residence at the University of Iowa, where he was also a visiting lecturer. He began to contribute pieces to popular magazines, but was unhappy and restless:

I felt I'd *been* to Iowa. I'd gotten a lot out of it, I'd liked it fine. But now I wasn't wrestling so well anymore. I was getting *beaten up*. I was feeling old, physically. I was *sick of* teaching. I didn't want to *do it anymore*. I was restless, aimless. We lived in four houses over a three year period in the same dull city, Iowa City. I thought I was gonna die a death of boredom.[10]

While in this mood Irving published his darkest novel, *The 158-Pound Marriage*. This was his best-reviewed novel, but also his worst seller—only 2,560 copies.[11]

In 1975, Irving returned to New England to teach at Mount Holyoke, and the following year he taught at the Bread Loaf Writers' Conference in Middlebury, Vermont. In 1976, Irving made another important move; angry at the way Random House had handled his books, he changed affiliation (with that former publisher's encouragement) to E. P. Dutton, where the late Henry Robbins had recently established his own editorial imprint.

The novel that Irving published with Robbins and E. P. Dutton was *The World According to Garp*, an enormous critical and commercial success, which made Irving suddenly a famous and popular literary figure. *Garp* sold over 100,000 copies in hardcover, and the paperback, released amid a large promotional campaign—featuring the slogan, "I Believe in Garp"—has sold more than three million copies. The novel was nominated for a National Book Award and received the American Book Award as the best paperback novel in 1979.

Irving's new celebrity status and wealth allowed him to retire from teaching and to concentrate on his writing, which he pursues at his homes in Putney, Vermont, and Cambridge, Massachusetts. His fifth novel, *The Hotel New Hampshire*, was published in the fall of 1981 by E. P. Dutton. Its appearance was preceded by much publicity, including a *Time* magazine cover story (August 31, 1981). The book was issued in a first printing of 150,000 copies.

Irving is currently at work on a new novel, which he plans to make short, very intense, and readable in one sitting. Taking Ivan Turgenev and Thomas Hardy as models for the use of landscape as a pervasive presence in the narrative, Irving projects a first-person account of a teenage boy's search for a family of his own. Irving also has been serving as an advisor for the film version of *The World According to Garp*, which is being directed by George Roy Hill from a script by Steve Tesich. The film is to be released by Warner Brothers in the fall of 1982.

John Irving's ideas about fiction are openly expli-cated in his novels and clearly defined in two essays, "Kurt Vonnegut and His Critics" and "In Defense of Sentimentality." Concerned with and considerate of his readers, he wants to be widely read and feels that it is the writer's responsibility to tell a good story well. He is very much against the post-modernist tendency in fiction and criticism to promote what is "difficult," academic, and consciously "important" over what is seemingly "easy," readable, and perhaps popular.

In his fiction Irving deplores the contemporary novel's dedication to form rather than content, its tendency to place greater emphasis on structural complexity than on character and society. In *The World According to Garp*, he ridicules this supra-literary vogue when an important literary journal turns down Garp's first story:

> *The story is only mildly interesting, and it does nothing new with language or with form. Thanks for showing it to us, though.*
>
> Garp was puzzled and he showed the rejection to Tinch. Tinch was also puzzled.

"I guess they're interested in n-n-*newer* fiction," Tinch said.

"What's that?" Garp asked.

Tinch admitted he didn't really know. "The new fiction is interested in language and in f-f-form, I guess," Tinch said. "But I don't understand what it's really about. Sometimes it's about it-it-itself, I think," Tinch said.

This tendency to prize the trendy and the stridently intellectual over more enduring values in fiction is taken up directly by Irving in his essay on Kurt Vonnegut, wherein Irving attacks those critics who dismiss Vonnegut as an artist because of the relative simplicity of his narratives:

> The assumption that what is easy to read has been easy to write is a forgivable lapse among non-writers, but it is self-incriminating how many critics, who also (in a fashion) write themselves, have called Vonnegut "easy." . . . I would say, however, that there are many "serious people who take fiction seriously" . . . who think that Pynchon's kind of writing is the easiest to write. And the hardest to read: a struggle with ideas and language where we, the readers, provide much of the struggle; where the writer, perhaps, has not struggled hard enough to make himself more readable.[12]

Being "easy" is intimately connected with being "readable." In the same essay on Vonnegut, he poses the question, "Why is readable such a bad thing to be these days?"—and then goes on to say:

> Some "serious people" I know are gratified by the struggle to make sense of what they read. . . . I am more often gratified by a writer who has accepted the enormous effort necessary to make writing clear.

Vonnegut's lucidity is hard and brave work in a literary world where pure messiness is frequently thought to be a sign of some essential wrestling with the "hard questions."[13]

Not only does a writer have the responsibility of clarity, but he must also be mimetic; the novel must have character and plot with which readers can identify and which are recognizable, as reflections of a tangible reality. And most important, the novelist must care enough about people to demonstrate in his fiction a commitment to life and to society, a feat to be accomplished only by writing about people, for people. Irving is fond of telling a story about a very bright graduate student who wrote an ingenious but essentially meaningless story:

> I had a student when I taught in Iowa and all the people out there thought he was brilliant. I agreed, he was brilliant to me, too. . . . He wrote this story about a three-course meal from the point of view of a fork. The fork was the main character. It was brilliant, no question about it. And everybody in the class said that it was the best story we had read all year.
> Well, there was this kid in the class from India, and his struggles with English were just beginnnng. . . . At the end of the class . . . the Indian stood up and said "Excuse me please, I cannot respond to this story, being not a fork." I thought, "Yeah, I know what you mean." And that's a point of view. You know, you risk nothing when you write a story like that. You are never going to be sentimental, you are not going to fall into a love trap, you are not going to be melodramatic, or lurid, or pornographic; you are not going to do any of the things you can be called up short for. No risk.[14]

That final comment not only reveals Irving's attitude toward his material, but also reflects upon his style. He is deliberately excessive and baroque, and he indeed takes risks. Garp and Jenny Fields, Siggy in *Setting Free the Bears,* the narrator of *The 158-Pound Marriage,* Merrill Overturf and Ralph Packer in *The Water-Method Man,* Franny in *The Hotel New Hampshire*—all are extreme personalities. The situations in which they are placed are often extreme ones, as well: Siggy's planning of the zoo break, the narrator's sexual experiments, Fred Trumper's association with the FBI, Garp's birth, the activities of the Ellen Jamesians, Robert Muldoon's sex-change experience. Then, too, the violence that characterizes the novels is extreme in circumstance and effect in such episodes as the Garps' driveway accident, Siggy's crashing into the crates of bees, the shower of glass falling on the Winters' children in a bathtub, or the decapitations in the Akthelt and Gunnel saga. Irving believes in finding truth through exaggeration; his vision is thus extreme. Like Philip Roth, Irving remarks on the current age as one which competes with the novelist —asked about the exaggeration in his fiction, he merely points to world events: "I don't think Ellen Jamesians are very far out at all, and nobody who has gone in to clean up the 910 bodies in Guyana, I could imagine, would think the Ellen Jamesians had much to offer to compare to that." He comments further:

> We are certainly now in a decade that is punctuated by extreme overreactions to things, and I think we are going to witness a lot more reaction and overreaction in the future, particularly in the sexual striving for equality. I think exaggeration in writing is simply a result of paying attention to the world around us.[15]

If Irving tends to concentrate on the extremes of violence and language, he also advocates sentimentality. In practice he unashamedly manipulates his audience, building up his audience's love for certain characters (especially in *Garp),* only to take them away abruptly, usually through violent death later in the novel. This is done quite self-consciously and deliberately, for Irving is very conscious of his role as entertainer and makes no attempt to deny or conceal the machinations of his storytelling. Irving greatly admires the willingness of Charles Dickens, one of his literary models, to indulge in sentiment, as well as his enormous generosity. (Dickens's devotion to his audience also endears him to Irving.) In an essay in *The New York Times Book Review,* Irving attacked the popular tendency to appreciate Dickens only during the Christmas season:

> It is surprising, however, how many readers reserve Dickens—and hopefulness is general—for Christmas; it seems that what we applaud in Dickens—his kindness, his generosity, his belief in our dignity—is also what we condemn him for (under another name) in the off-Christmas season.
>
> The other name is sentimentality—and, to the modern reader, too often when a writer risks being sentimental, the writer is already guilty.[16]

Irving concludes his remarks by recommending the rediscovery, by readers and writers alike, of a rather neglected, though timeless and touching example of the old master's art:

> But this Christmas, since we're so familiar with "A Christmas Carol"—in its several versions—we might well read "Great Expectations"; it is a book many of us read last when we were in school, when we were too young to appreciate it. For its Christmas spirit—its open-hearted and forgiving qualities, and its feast of language—it is the best of novels by a writer of no mincing art.
>
> And when we writers—in our own work—escape

the slur of sentimentality, we should ask ourselves if what we are doing matters.[17]

All this sounds very moral, and Irving—though he is a little uncomfortable with the label—is a moral writer; even John Gardner names him as "one of the up and coming moral writers."[18] Like Dickens, Irving consistently demonstrates a generous and vital concern for humanity, and unlike many of his contemporaries, his is an art of engagement, one concerned with man's public and private responsibility to himself and others. Irving emphasizes these qualities in analyzing his own artistic temperament:

I feel that I am a very life-affirming person. I mean, of course, I believe in blackness, you would be an idiot not to, you see it everywhere; but at the same time, I believe that literature is a sign of life, not a sign of death. If a novel doesn't say something about human value, there isn't any worth in it.[19]

This is most apparent in his most recent work, *The Hotel New Hampshire*, wherein Irving shifts fictional gears, writing his novel as a fairy tale, subordinating characterization to symbolic structure and, in so doing, evoking some basic storytelling patterns. Finding his own world moving ever closer to spiritual disintegration, and alarmed at the failure of much art to come to grips with that threat, Irving provides a setting of magic and dreams, from which to make a direct appeal to the soul and the imagination. His tale, then, builds to a transcendent vision of a family's progress toward maturity, stability, and a measure of happiness.

In his last three novels—and most pointedly in *Garp*—Irving is very much concerned with the imagination and the imaginative process. According to Garp,

> . . . The autobiographical basis—if there even was one
> —was the least interesting level on which to read a
> novel. He would always say that the art of fiction was
> the act of *imagining* truly—was, like any art, a process of
> selection. Memories and personal histories—"all the
> recollected traumas of our unmemorable lives"—were
> suspicious models for fiction. . . .

Some of that novel's critics, dealing with the book upon its publication, were confused by, or misunderstood, that statement, primarily because T. S. Garp was confused with John Irving. Despite the autobiographical similarities—and there are many, including the New England prep school education, the stay in Vienna, wrestling, and the subjects of two of their novels—Garp is not Irving. The careful reader will notice that there are important differences between Garp's *Procrastination* and *Second Wind of the Cuckold* and Irving's *Setting Free the Bears* and *The 158-Pound Marriage* (see Chapter 5). Also, the autobiographical parallels are only of the sketchiest nature, which is not to deny that there is a strong autobiographical element in Irving's work—clearly it is there, though Irving himself is often petulant on this subject in interviews. He is right to discourage preoccupation with the search for parallels between his protagonists' lives and his own and to turn attention to other aspects of his art, but Irving uses his personal history too often to allow us to dismiss it, and it is important to note his apparent need to use it. In *The Water-Method Man*, for example, Irving describes his hero's life in details that nearly parallel his own: born on the same day as Irving, Fred Trumper, too, graduates from Exeter; is on the wrestling team there; attends the Universities of Pittsburgh, New Hampshire, and Iowa; and even marries in the same year as Irving did (1964).[20]

Biography, then, is important, and, as Irving insists in *Setting Free the Bears,* so is history—if Irving really believed that the novelist had to produce a work solely rooted in the imagination, all of his novels would have to be considered failures. His practical aesthetic credo, however, is one of balance between elements of actual experience and invention, rather than the exclusion of either. Indeed, Garp's major artistic problem is that during his very short career he deals too much in extremes, as Irving points out in an interview:

> Garp went from totally imaginative writing to almost autobiographical, with the addition of sordid details, . . . Then, after *Bensenhaver,* he had reached a point where he had found his vision; he had figured out how to write so that he could combine the details in his life with his imagination and come up with what he was trying to write.[21]

This is what Irving had tried to achieve in his own work, the use of autobiography and history as a groundwork and basis upon which to build imaginative constructs. His novels involve a progressive reworking of certain materials, an attempt each time to distance himself further from them and to see what can be made of them. Irving and his characters regularly confront the past not only to try to understand it but also to search it for some imaginative connection or fusion of present and past in order to make something of their lives. In Irving's world, this quest is required as a prelude to the commission of any significant gesture, such as Hannes' decision to free the bears; Trumper's determination to marry

Tulpen; or Garp's metamorphosis into a true writer, father, and husband.

For Irving, then, "the recollected traumas" are useful. The recollections are all part of "imagining truly," for it is when the writer can deal with his recollections in an imaginative way that he truly shapes his vision—Irving thus ascribes to the Wordsworthian concept of poetry's origin as "emotion recollected in tranquillity." The narrator's failure in *The 158-Pound Marriage* and Garp's failures, in fact, originate in the tendency to write in the heat of passion, without the proper emotional distance. And when Irving's own writing achieves its greatest power, he manages to combine aspects of his life or the history that fascinates him with, in Wordsworth's words, "a certain colouring of imagination, . . . whereby ordinary things should be presented to the mind in an unusual aspect; and further, and above all, to make these incidents and situations interesting by tracing in them, truly though not ostentatiously, the primary laws of our nature. . . ."[22]

It is in this light that "The Dog in the Alley" episode in *Garp* must be understood. Garp first tells his son Walt a bedtime story about how a dog, tied on a chain to the front axle of an old army truck, plots revenge against a cat that is always teasing him, concluding the tale with the death of the dog. After Walt is asleep, Garp's wife, Helen, suspecting that there may be an element of truth in the story, questions Garp about it. He then teases her by offering different versions, constantly inventing variations on the basic story, some version of which he did actually witness in Vienna. In so doing, he demonstrates the artist's basic process of building on reality and using his imagination to construct a better story than the one that actually happened, striving for the invention that seems most "truthful." Irving's narrator explains:

> Garp never tired of playing this game, though Helen certainly tired of it. He would wait for her to ask: . . . Which of it is true, which of it is made up? Then he would say to her that it didn't matter; she would just tell him what she didn't *believe*. Then he would change that part. Every part she believed was true; every part she didn't believe needed work.

In the same vein, Garp remarks to an interviewer in the novel, "Tell me anything that's ever happened to you . . . and I can improve upon the story; I can make the details better than they were."

In other words, the writer is totally absorbed and obsessed by his own vision of reality; he rules it and controls it. In Irving's world facts and histories are recorded, rejected, repeated, shaped, and reshaped. The purpose is not only to test the material and so arrive at a truth, but for Irving it is even more important to transform a violent, chaotic, haphazard world into a configuration of some shape and form—ultimately, that is, an environment that can be controlled. As Garp says, "fiction has to be better made than life."

In *The Hotel New Hampshire* Irving returns to the world of "The Pension Grillparzer," shaping a wholly imaginative landscape. Both works are narrated by central male characters and are essentially family stories. Both are about ways of viewing life: the world of childhood innocence is magical and full of wonders, as the child's imagination is able to assimilate mundane occurrences as well as bears that ride on motorcycles or unicycles and men who walk on their hands. But even this vision does not remain ideal, for in Irving's world the specter of death is always near. In "The Pension Grillparzer" it appears in the form of the grandmother's dream; in *The Hotel New Hampshire* a man in a white dinner jacket delivers cryptic warnings of death and destruction.

As discussed in more detail later (Chapter 5), Irving's vision is markedly different from Garp's. In "Pension" the final emphasis falls on doom and death because the narrator is too far removed from the imaginative gleam of his childhood to be able to see the world as other than "a doomed effort at reclassification"; this is a limitation in Garp's vision as well. Irving, on the other hand, demonstrates in his fifth novel that reclassification can succeed. The conclusion of *The Hotel New Hampshire* reverts to the magical universe of the novel's opening—a world where a bear may change into a woman and where the narrator and his family can triumph over death and recollected trauma. Irving goes beyond the Romantics in asserting the validity of the imagination and our ability to reclaim it even in adulthood—even in the world of "experience."

John Irving's world (with the exception of that reflected in his first novel) is an insular one; his heroes are generally enmeshed in private or familial problems, so absorbed in themselves, and the reader in them, that other dimensions cease to be very important. The "real world," in the form of actual historical or sociological events, does not intrude. Irving does not make reference to the events of his time to give his works background or to ground them in a precise historical framework, nor does he strive for strict sociological realism. With the exception of *Setting Free the Bears*, which is totally concerned with a particular historical moment, only *The 158-Pound Marriage* directly refers to a "current event"—the narrator and his wife return to America on the day of John F. Kennedy's assassination.

Nevertheless, Irving's novels are very much products of their time, and if the reader is not clued in with specific references to history, there is yet enough "felt reality" to give the novels a striking and dramatic sense of verisimilitude. The assassinations in *Garp* (especially that of Jenny Fields), the psychic dislocation of Fred Trumper, the descriptions of the artistic community of Greenwich Village, and the descriptions of the cinema verité of Ralph Packer in *The Water-Method Man*—all communicate a profound and sensitive impression of their time.

Irving's world is not so insular, however, that outside forces do not make their presence known. In fact, Irving's universe is largely governed by mishap, violence, and the irrational. In *Garp* Irving concretizes this force, calling it the Under Toad, but it is, indeed, everywhere in his fiction. All his protagonists' lives are continually disrupted by minor annoyances, domestic squabbles, or psychological problems. The Under Toad is at its most frightening, however, when it erupts into violence and death. Each of Irving's novels contains at least one central violent episode, and two of them, *Setting Free the Bears* and *Garp,* are even dominated by death—virtually everyone dies by each novel's conclusion.

The basic problem for Irving's characters is determining how to conduct their lives in the face of such chaos—how does one live in a world ruled by the Under Toad? Irving offers no clear-cut solutions, but he does suggest some support systems, and here again his practice is to be distinguished from some prominent tendencies of his contemporaries. The emphasis on the individual caught up in an absurd and irrational universe is the central theme of modern fiction. Despite Irving's emphasis on the mingling of comedy with death and tragedy, however, he is not, as has been suggested, a black humorist. The concentration on forces rather than on individuals, and the lack of real engagement in characterization that is common to writers of that genre, are alien to Irving. The black humorist's vision is one that does not allow his protagonists victory or real reconciliation, either with family or with society; unlike traditional comedy, which celebrates the victory of life over death, black humor stops short of such affirmation. Irving's characters, on the other hand, though they recognize the forces of what Celine calls this "truly appalling and awful world," must refuse to yield to it or to be paralyzed by it. They learn to recognize the Under Toad and to live with it, not through passive acceptance but with vigorous defiance. Thus, Irving is actually closer to the existential vision of Camus than to the black humorists—his characters do choose and do act, and even if an action like setting free the bears seems a futile one, it serves as a way of combatting the Under Toad by asserting the self.

Achieving this state of selfhood and reconciliation is difficult, and Irving's characters go through many moments of despair, paralysis, guilt, and pain before achieving wholeness. One way to battle the Under Toad is to understand history, and *Setting Free the Bears* is Irving's attempt to present this possibility. Unlike some contemporary novelists' attempts at rewriting history (E. L. Doctorow's *Ragtime*, Robert Coover's *The Public Burning*) in order to reshape it or transcend it—and in the process, reject it—Irving's historical novel is quite faithful to facts and events, for he does not want to turn away from history, but to confront it. In doing so, Irving concentrates on World War II, the event that is primarily responsible for the shaping of our age, and focuses on the *Anschluss* (a public failure of courage and of principle) and the Yugoslavian civil wars (a kind of private failure). History is intimately related to Irving's use of Vienna, which functions at the same time as a real and a symbolic place in his novels. In many ways Vienna is the central character in *Setting Free the Bears;* a place of occupation, power, intrigue, poverty, and ruin, it is certainly more vital than the human characters. Through the exploration of its essence, Siggy and Hannes are finally able to come to an understanding of the larger world. Postwar Vienna, with its profound sense of romantic desperation, its linguistic and ethnic mix, also influences the lives of Severin Winter and Utch, Garp, and Bogus Trumper, and especially in *The Hotel New Hampshire,* it becomes a place of moral corruption and destruction, where the norms of civilized behavior are blurred. It is where the lessons of the Under Toad are crystallized.

Finally, successful characters, like Hannes, Severin Winter, Garp, and John Berry, come to an understanding of these larger, public issues of life, but the private aspect is also very important, and Irving's novels generally concentrate on the family. *The Water-Method Man* and *Garp* are primarily family novels, as both Trumper and Garp must come to understand their roles as husbands and fathers before they can successfully practice the more public roles of teacher and writer. *The Hotel New Hampshire,* more than any of the novels, concentrates on the family almost to the exclusion of history—insisting on the individual's responsibility to himself and others and the necessity of integrating the various aspects of the personality. Achieving selfhood through a strong marriage and devotion to true parenting is presented as the best hope for triumphing over the forces of chaos and despair. *The 158-Pound Marriage,* on the other hand, combines the public and the private in nearly equal parts—like *Setting Free the Bears,* it tackles modern European history, and like the other novels, it is concerned with the family. The narrator of that novel, a historical novelist, is Irving's only out-and-out failure, a man who fails to understand both history and himself.

Most of Irving's characters, however, do achieve victory, reconciling themselves to family, society, and history and learning to recognize and to grapple with the Under Toad. Hannes in *Setting Free the Bears* learns the lesson of history from Siggy's journal, and by the end of the novel he is ready to ride out on the open road and deal with the world. Fred Trumper comes to accept his familial responsibility and the death of his closest friend, and at last is comforted by "all the good flesh around him." Severin Winter and Utch are able to utilize their deprived childhoods as orphans of war to come to an understanding of their needs and responsibilities as members of a family. Garp triumphs over profound loss and his own selfish arrogance and so moves toward both artistic and emotional liberation. John Berry overcomes the traumatic experience of Vienna and his passionate love for his sister to become a true husband and father and the central agent of his family's future.

Many of Irving's characters achieve wholeness by returning to the scene of childhood: Garp to the Steering School (where he will die), Utch and Severin Winter to Vienna, Trumper to Maine—always a restorative place in Irving's work—where, with his childhood friends, his ex-wife and son, and his new family, he conducts an elaborate ceremony to celebrate his life's renewal. In this sense Irving's novels regularly exhibit a cyclical, timeless quality that is most poetically developed in the return to primal beginnings in *The Hotel New Hampshire,* which begins and ends in a fairy-tale world. That novel concludes in Maine, where Father's story began and where John, the true father, awaits the arrival of the child that is to be both the symbol and the fruition of his family's survival.

Another means of such triumph is art, for most of Irving's earlier protagonists are writers: Siggy writes a journal in which he tries to analyze his family and World War II; Trumper writes a journal to try to piece together his life; the narrator of *The 158-Pound Marriage* writes novels, and *The 158-Pound Marriage* itself is, in part, his attempt to come to grips with the *ménage a quatre* of which he was a part; Garp is also a novelist. Irving thus asserts that one way to deal with life is to shape it, control it, and give it form, so that some understanding can be reached. Art is indispensable in the fight against the Under Toad.

Another important weapon is laughter. All of Irving's novels are comic, and all of them contain sections that are marvelously funny. Irving is not laughing at his characters, however; in a sense he is laughing back at the forces that threaten them. And, ultimately, most of his characters find the strength to laugh with him. If Siggy, Trumper, Garp, and the Berrys cannot defeat the Under Toad, they can learn to stand back and defy its power to destroy their lives—in Irving's world such laughter is therapeutic. An exuberant, playful spirit pervades all the novels, manifesting the joy that Irving must have felt in inventing the broad situations in which he places his characters, and although events do turn out badly much of the time, he has yet mastered the delicate art of mingling laughter with compassion, "lunacy and sorrow." If Irving must cause his characters and readers much pain and sorrow, he is also extremely generous and forgiving, and if he insists that we face difficult and disturbing truths, it is only because we must know them to survive.

Irving's generosity and his emphasis on freedom, laughter, and fun balance the harsher aspects of his vision and provide an important prescription for survival in this world. As Terence Des Pres writes, "All comic artists are tricksters. They skate on thin ice, they make us laugh, they help us to hang on. And the survival value of laughter, in times like ours, cannot be too highly prized."[23]

# CHAPTER 2

# In the Vienna Woods

Irving's first novel, *Setting Free the Bears*, is his weakest, although it remains interesting as an introductory treatment of themes and motifs that Irving would develop further in his later works. Most importantly, this novel details the framework for Irving's world view, which makes it essential to an understanding of his art. In this novel is found his most thorough examination of the Austrian history (specifically, the *Anschluss*) and the Austrian setting that figures prominently in all of his books. *Setting Free the Bears* is a rarity among American novels in that it is set completely in Europe and has no American characters. Irving's later, American, novels, however, have no real, identifiable settings; the places are named, but they are not felt, and no real sense of them is conveyed. Vienna, indeed, is the only place that is strongly evoked in Irving's fiction, and most deliberately so in this early novel. Not until *The World According to Garp* is Irving to deal with the city in such detail again, as his protagonist recreates Vienna imaginatively in his story "The Pension Grillparzer."

*Setting Free the Bears* is divided into three parts:

the first introduces the two central characters, Siegfried (Siggy) Javotnick and Hannes Graff, two drop-
outs from the University of Vienna who spend a
carefree time loose on the European landscape on
their 700-cc. Royal Enfield motorcycle. During this
time they are dreaming up a plan to liberate the
animals from Vienna's Hietzinger Zoo. The second
part, entitled "The Notebook"—the novel's most fully
sustained narrative section—provides a history of
Siggy's parents, whose lives were profoundly affected
both by Austria's capitulation to Hitler in 1938 and by
the period of internal struggle in Yugoslavia between
the German army, Tito's partisans, and a Croatian
terrorist group. This tale, in turn, is interspersed with
Siggy's notes on his zoo watch, taken from a diary he
kept while formulating his plans to free the animals.
The final section deals primarily with the zoo break
itself.

The novel's first and last sections constitute a
rather conventional coming-of-age story, employing
the picaresque form that is common to many novels
of youthful escape (a popular enough formula in
American fiction). Irving's young rebels yearn for
and achieve, in part, the joyful freedom associated
with life on the road. As is also fairly common among
works in this form, however, their story suffers from
a central weakness in characterization. Both protagonists remain essentially one-dimensional, so flat that it
is often difficult to distinguish them. It is established
that Siggy is the more idealistic (the zoo bust is his
obsession) and carefree of the two, but that is all. At
times they seem to exist as mere pawns for whom
Irving can invent broad comic adventures, rarely, if
ever, suggesting that they have lives or thoughts of
their own. This weakness is most apparent in the
abrupt conclusion of the first section (the first of
Irving's violent climactic sequences, which will be-

come a stylistic trademark)—when Siggy is killed while trying to escape the police, crashing into a wagon load of honey-filled beehives, the reader, after spending one hundred pages "on the road" with him, is likely to feel no loss or sadness at his death.

Irving also fails to place his "flower children" within any convincing social context. Generally the progress of the picaresque rogue is a counterpoint and commentary on the society through which he moves, but Irving conveys no real idea of the society from which his heroes are in flight—the fact that they are "at loose ends" is not enough. The novel, which is very much a product of the 1960s, seems to be playing upon the reader's assumptions about that particular era, but a novelist cannot rely entirely on such assumptions. In his notebook, Siggy complains,

> That's a bit of what you live with if you're 21 in 1967, in Austria; you don't have a history, really, and no immediate future that you can see. What I mean is, we're at an interim age in an interim time; we're alive between two times of monstrous decisions—one past, the other coming. We're taking up the lag in history, for who knows how long.

Beyond this, the narrative attempts to create no tangible sense of this "age." What makes it an interim time? What is Austria like in 1967? Irving offers no clues.

Siggy is himself preoccupied with history, as the journal, which he calls his "Prehistory," indicates—this was to have been his thesis at the university, but was rejected for having no footnotes. Nevertheless, his rendering of the events that make up his emotional past is very perceptive, despite his claim that it is not real history. Indeed, it is unfortunate that the rational, reflective Siggy who is revealed through his journal does not more deeply influence the Siggy portrayed in Part One. This erratic rebel's plan to set the animals free is to be his attempt to make history, by performing a supposedly significant act in an insignificant time, and perhaps, to rectify some of the errors recorded in his Prehistory. The action of Part One functions also as a kind of counterpoint to the Prehistory, as Siggy seeks frantically to exploit his freedom "on the road," while attempting to defy danger, entrapment, and death. His freedom, however, like any in Irving's world, can be only temporary. His death ends his active participation, although Hannes, his reluctant disciple, will eventually carry out the plan for him. (Siggy's fate is the first indication of that element of mishap which frequently intrudes in Irving's universe, sometimes, as in Siggy's case, fatally—even in peacetime his characters are continually under siege by forces that seem to conspire against them.)

The first section, entitled "Siggy," is narrated in the first person by Hannes, and it is a sad example of apparent comic intent undercut by forced humor and stilted wit. Siggy and Hannes, deciding that Vienna is "no spot for the spring," buy a motorcycle and take to the road, their attitude summarized by one of Siggy's aphorisms (which Hannes sprinkles throughout the narrative): "Be blissfully guided by the veritable urge!" (Irving's use of sayings from notebooks will recur, with greater success, in *Garp.*) The rules they live by are "no planning," "pick roads the beast will love," and "travel light." They begin their journey by buying flowers and tossing them to girls on the street, but before leaving the city, they decide to stop at the zoo. Here the reader is introduced to the "Famous Asiatic Black Bears," symbolic in the novel of ultimate brutality, and described as "unfamiliar with compromise." This species will later be contrasted with the

"Rare Spectacled Bears" who represent the more socializing impulses of harmony and appeasement.

In a more general sense, bears regularly serve, in Irving's works, as symbolic representations of various human states of captivity and freedom, which are central concepts in this first novel. The opposed characteristics of the two species—the wild rebelliousness of the Famous Asiatic Black Bears versus the tamer, almost domestic placidity of the Rare Spectacled Bears—suggest basic instincts that are polarized, perhaps uneasily, in the unnatural habitat of organized society. As Irving has taken pains to emphasize, he refers always to bears in captivity, trained or caged in zoos[1]—animals held in controlled environments from which he and/or his characters frequently imagine them released, "set free" upon a world unfamiliar and seemingly unstructured. The juxtaposition of this bear mythology, as stressed in Siggy's narrative and in his schemes for the zoo break, to the specific historical events outlined in his Prehistory, provides an evocative, if sometimes elusive, reflection upon the experiences and the personalities of the various national "species" involved in the turmoil of wartime. The fierce independence of the Yugoslav tribes contrasts directly to the nearly inert complacency of the Austrian people, both, in effect, pressured into a choice of freedom or captivity by the imperialist advances of the Germans, who had been, in turn, "loosed" from their traditional boundaries—and the Prussian bear is a familiar national symbol—by Hitler. Once "set free" from the civilized constraints of their former political situations, these various peoples reacted to the prospects of such freedom in different ways, producing a resultant state of chaos from which the world has not yet really recovered.

The illusion of freedom which Irving's two motorcycle riders pursue is tested at every turn in a

series of slapstick encounters. The first comes in a
chapter ironically titled "Living off the Land"—Siggy
and Hannes have gone back to basics, camping out
under the stars and fishing for their dinner. As they
prepare for bed the first evening, Siggy begins thinking of freeing the animals:

> *"How* nice!" said Siggy, "And the oryx! Can't you see
> him wading across the river, dipping those fantastic
> balls?"
> "Freeze them off," I said.
> "No!" said Siggy. *"Nothing* could damage that
> oryx!"

The oryx is another metaphor for freedom, this time
sexual. Siggy is, of course, wrong—all things are
doomed to be "damaged"—which is something he
should have learned from history.

The next morning Siggy and Hannes catch
twelve trout, which they hope to trade for some
breakfast, and they find willing customers at a nearby
farm who give them coffee and potatoes in exchange.
In his enthusiasm, Siggy remarks, "And we're just
starting out at this business. . . . Living off the land.
. . . Back to the simple laws of nature." One of the
customers, a game warden, replies, "You would have
to go and remind me of *laws,*" and regretfully fines
them fifty schillings for catching more than their
limit. In 1967, "the laws of nature" are no longer
either simple or even natural—unlike Thoreau, who
can earn his living "by the labor of my hands only,"
Siggy and Hannes can never retreat far enough away
from the restricting laws of society. Siggy takes revenge this time by stealing some utensils from his
hosts, including a frying pan, saying, "There are
certain investments required . . . if one is to live off
the land."

In another incident that prefigures the zoo bust, Siggy frees some penned-up goats, which causes a bit of panic in the town of Hiesbach, where the goats go up the steps to the church door. Siggy, however, is frustrated that they won't "bolt." As Siggy and Hannes leave the town, the goats are being rounded up, and the final image they are left with is rather pathetic:

> The first goat was on its feet, but a fat girl had it in a headlock and its beard was ratily plucked.
> Its pink mouth was open for bleating, but we couldn't hear it calling us over the motorcycle.

Again, Siggy should have known—what can a freed animal do in the middle of a modern city or town? In Hiesbach or Vienna, animals are better off in the zoo.

Siggy's next encounter with an animal sets in motion the events that lead to his death. While on the road Siggy and Hannes pick up a girl named Gallen, who joins them on the motorcycle. While holding on to her, Hannes slips and burns his legs on the motorcycle's pipes: "The pipes received my calves like the griddle grabs the bacon."—it is the first of many such intrusions of danger and pain during a moment of seeming serenity in Irving's fiction. Hannes is taken by Gallen to her aunt's *Gasthof* to recuperate. One morning Siggy witnesses there a milkman beating and mistreating his horse: "Then he pounded the horse's head on the cobblestones; he just tugged it up by the ears and flung it down again, leaning his weight after it. The horse's forehooves began to flay through the rain." Siggy leaps to the horse's rescue and beats the milkman. When the police are called, Siggy manages to escape capture. He will spend the next few days in Vienna planning the zoo break before returning for his friend.

Hannes, meanwhile, is ordered by the police to get a job or be arrested for vagrancy. Accepting the task of "bringing in the bees" whose hives are full, he imagines he hears "the dungeon door closing with terrible wrenching clanks; and deep in my ears, sounding all the way from Vienna, the Rare Spectacled Bears were stamping their feet and shaking their heads with a fury that flapped their jowls." In denying the animal in himself, Hannes becomes in part responsible for Siggy's death.

Siggy dies when he comes to retrieve Hannes, who is working with the bees. Trying to escape Keff, who supervises Hannes, the two fugitives crash the motorcycle into a wagon full of honey-filled beehives, crushing Siggy underneath. Irving's world is constantly disrupted by the irrational, which appears usually in the form of extreme violence, as when a delirious Hannes recalls his helplessness after the accident:

> I heard you. I came running. And I would have gotten there if the bees hadn't closed my eyes, filled my ears and slowed me to a crawl. Even then I might have gotten there, if Keff hadn't come lumbering down on me, taking me over his hip and up under his arm and bumbling me back up the road.

As Hannes sinks into unconsciousness, he once again hears the sounds of the animals and the bears mourning the death of a wild and free spirit.

This incident has been prefigured ironically by Irving earlier, when Siggy comments on some bees pollinating apple buds: "Isn't fertilization grand." Hannes thinks, "Well, the bees make honey for the beekeeper, the bees multiply the orchard man's apples, no one's hurt by that." In the world of Irving, however, "hurt" is always lurking somewhere, as Siggy, despite his idealism, recognizes in one of his poems: "Fate waits./ While you hurry/ Or while you wait,/ It's all the same to Fate." In another, similar, poem Siggy writes: "Disaster, disaster,/ We're having a/ Disaster./ If we try to/ Get away,/ Disaster/ Will run faster."

Siggy has a certain, albeit imperfect, knowledge of history. His more cynical but tempered sensibility separates him from Hannes, who has a great deal to learn. For it is Hannes who must grow and stumble into manhood and self-awareness during the course of the novel. His brief entanglement with Siggy and his reading of Siggy's notebook will teach him certain lessons about how things work in the world according to John Irving.

Siggy's Prehistory is, in essence, a meditation on history as revealed through the experiences of his parents. It is also a further elaboration on the concept of freedom. Part of the narrative begins in Austria in 1938, just prior to Hitler's takeover, and concludes in 1955 at the end of the Russian occupation of Vienna.

The history is presented in a serio-comic vein; like Vonnegut's Billy Pilgrim, the reader becomes "unstuck in time." However, Irving's characters are not sent to a fictional planet, but made to bear witness to a public and very real catastrophe. Irving's preoccupation with Austria and the *Anschluss* is significant because it is based on a recognition that this was the beginning of the horror that was to become the postmodern world, the forerunner of the escalation to the Holocaust, Hiroshima, and the Cold War. As Gordon Brook-Shepherd has written, "The *Anschluss* . . . was the real beginning of Armageddon."[2]

Irving details significant events of the Nazi take-over of Austria, beginning with the assassination of Chancellor Engelbert Dollfuss in 1934, which is referred to in Siggy's narrative and remains permanently in the story's background, for it triggered the collapse to come. Dollfuss was a strong political leader who had eliminated the various Austrian political parties and established the Fatherland Front to combat the Nazi party. The assassin sent by Hitler was Otto Planetta, who was promptly hanged by Dollfuss's replacement, Kurt von Schuschnigg, much to Hitler's displeasure. Also mentioned in the narrative is this new leader's conference with Hitler at Berchtesgaden, at which, through compromise and an inability to stand up to Hitler, Schuschnigg bartered away Austria's independence. Schuschnigg agreed to appoint five Nazis to his cabinet, including Artur Seyss-Inquart, who had become his greatest political enemy. Compromise was always a major factor in Austria's history, hardly unique to Schuschnigg, who also believed in loyalty to Germany, and who, up to the meeting at Berchtesgaden, was unaware of Hitler's maniacal ambitions.

Against this background, an Austrian named Zahn Glanz courts Hilke Marter, the mother of Siggy. Two other fictional characters figure prominently in this part of the Prehistory: Siggy's grandfather, who seems to have a profound sense of Austrian history, and Ernst Watzek-Trummer, a farmer who will develop one. The immediate social background is Schuschnigg's announcement of a plebiscite, the voters to decide between an independent Austria and union with Germany. Irving parallels this announcement with an example of the decadent behavior that was characteristic of the period, as a radio announcer reports:

> . . . a young woman identified as Mara Madoff . . . was found this morning hanging in her coat on a coat hook in the second-balcony wardrobe closet of the Vienna State Opera House. . . . Authorities attribute the cause of death to a star-shaped series of fine-pointed stab wounds in the heart, and estimate the time of death as well toward the end of the opera. The authorities say that the young woman was in no way assaulted; however, her stockings were missing and her shoes had been put back on. . . .

Zahn, an idealistic patriot, feels that the plebiscite is a good thing, but Grandfather Marter knows better. He realizes that what the people want means nothing: "I want a man who'll do what he says he'll do. And that was Dollfuss, and he got murdered by some of those *nobodies* you mention. And now we've got Schuschnigg, that's what we've got."

It remains for Ernst Watzek-Trummer to perform the supreme patriotic act in the novel's most fully realized comic sequence—he makes an eagle suit out of chicken feathers and pie plates, puts it on, and heads for the city. Here he walks around crying for a free Austria: "The vision with the terrifying wingspan clatters its feathered pieplate breast. 'Cawk! it cries. Cawk! Cawk! Austria is free!' And very slowly, after an awesome silence, drinkers, one by one, rush to embrace the national symbol." This act touches the Marter family, and Watzek-Trummer is embraced by Zahn and Grandfather Marter. Zahn even rides Ernst around in his taxi, and together they spread the message of freedom. Ernst knows, however, that his gesture is futile; he tells Zahn, "There won't be any vote. . . . They'll never get away with it, you young fool."

Ernst is right, of course, for on Black Friday, March 11, 1938, Austria will fall. Hitler phones

Schuschnigg and tells him to postpone the plebiscite;
Göring then forces Schuschnigg to resign and to
nominate Seyss-Inquart for the chancellorship. Irving undercuts the severity of these incidents with a
humor that borders on cynicism: "Göring has such an
odd way of putting things. He promises that Austria
will have German military aid, if the Schuschnigg
government cannot change itself promptly." Schuschnigg does resign, and his final act is described by
Irving in words that both condemn Schuschnigg and
yet recognize his untenable position:

> Then Kurt von Schuschnigg performs the last and
> most conclusive leap backwards of his career—an exec-
> utive order to General Schilhawsky to withdraw the
> Austrian Army from the German border; to offer no
> resistance; to watch, or perhaps wave, from behind the
> River Enns. The Austrian Army has only forty-eight
> hours of steady-fire ammunition anyway. What would
> be the point of so much blood? Someone phones from
> Salzburg to say the Germans are crossing the border;
> it's not true, it's a false alarm, but it's another fine hair
> to be split and Schuschnigg doesn't wait for verifica-
> tion. He steps back.

While all of this is going on, Zahn Glanz dresses in
Ernst's eagle suit and attempts once more to keep
Austria's hopes alive: "No such heavy thoughts are
weighing down Zahn Glanz. He's a bird and flying."
On the streets he is met by either indifference or
hostility and finally arrives at the Marter apartment
sick and exhausted.

On March 12, 1938, Seyss-Inquart becomes
chancellor of Austria and feels that all is in control.
Again, Irving undercuts this: "Poor Seyss-Inquart, he
should know better: if you bring lions to your home,
they'll want to stay for dinner." While Seyss-Inquart

drives Schuschnigg home, "to ten weeks of house arrest and seven years in Gestapo prisons," Grandfather Marter, his family, and Ernst Watzek-Trummer pack Zahn's taxi for their escape to Kaprun. Zahn stays behind, and in his last act of heroism (as is later speculated), drives an anti-Hitler newspaper editor over the border, for he is never heard of again. Siggy concludes that even though Zahn Glanz did not father him, "something of Zahn Glanz certainly got into me. I only want to show how Zahn Glanz put an idea of me in my mother. Even if he put nothing else there."

The next part of Siggy's history deals with his real father, Vratno Javotnik. Here Irving switches his attention to Yugoslavia, describing in his most savage tones, the genocide, class hatred, and the pointless civil strife that dominated Yugoslavia during the early stages of the war. Three central internal groups were fighting among themselves, as well as against the Germans and others. The Cetniks (or Chetniks, Anglicized), led by Colonel Drazha Mihailovich, were a Serbian guerrilla resistance force that attacked German units. Prominent in resisting the German occupation and in vehemently protesting the postwar situation of Communism in Yugoslavia, Mihailovich was hunted down and executed by the Tito government in 1946. In 1942, however, he had performed an act of great heroism, stubbornly refusing to accept the Nazi conquest of Yugoslavia:

> So the German onslaught against this upstart revolution was fierce. So fierce that on May 4 Germany announced that the Yugoloslav State was nonexistent. But on May 10, Colonel Drazha Mihailovich and his band of wild Chetniks hoisted the Yugoslav flag on the mountain of Ravna Gora. Mihailovich and his freedom fanatics went on doing that kind of thing all summer.

The second group were the Ustashi, pro-Nazi Croatian terrorists. They were headed by the Fascist Ante Pavelich, who was probably responsible for the assassination of King Alexander. Supported by fascist Italy, their actions greatly contributed to the breakup of Yugoslavia. The third group were the Communist partisans, led by Josip Broz (Tito), who originally supported the Chetniks against the Germans and who, Irving writes, "were fighting along with the Chetniks against the Germans when they weren't fighting against the Chetniks. [Tito] fought with Mihailovich before he turned against him."

This is the background against which Vratno Javotnik, Siggy's father, makes his spiritual odyssey. He aspires only to be a survivor; politics means nothing to him, except as it may serve his own personal needs: "I believe he was the only Yugoslav to whom being a Serb instead of a Croat wouldn't have made any difference—and splitting the hair between Croats and Slovenes would have been absurd for him. His politics were strictly personal." Vratno, however, becomes involved with the Slivinca family, who are part of the Ustashi terrorist group; he is assigned to dispose of Gottlob Wut, a German and the head of a motorcycle unit.

Absurdly enough, the Ustashi are uncertain exactly what they have against Wut—he is suspected of tinkering with an Italian racer before the Italian Grand Prix of 1930, allowing the NSU (German) motorcycle to win:

> Unfortunately, the Italian counterpart of the Ustashi had backed a number of syndicates who put their money on Guido Maggiacomo and his highly touted Velocette. When the betting turnover was tabulated, it appeared that the NSU team . . . had made a killing.

But the record has it that all the betting was done by the mystical mechanic Gottlob Wut. It was Wut who took away the booty.

As a linguist, adept at various languages, among them German—"This may have been a premonition on his part—pessimism at a tender age; to master the speech of several occupying armies before they came to occupy"—Vratno seems qualified for the job. However, while Vratno is getting to know Wut, this apolitical agent grows fond of his appointed victim and instead warns him of the Ustashi's intentions. Wut and Vratno then escape, but not before Wut blows up a car containing the Slivincas. Hiding out in the mountains and living off the land, the fugitives even join up for a while with a group of Chetniks on their way to meet Mihailovich. The civil strife, clearly, is becoming so confused that it is difficult to know who the good guys are. Wut understands the situation, however, and diagnoses it as purely a matter of propaganda:

> "Mihailovich is a goner," Wut said. "The trouble with Chetniks and all those fool Serbs is that they've got no idea of propaganda. They don't even have a party line—not so much as a slogan! There's nothing to grab on to. Now these partisans," said Wut, "they've got the radio controls, and a simple, unswerving line: defend Russia; communism is anti-Nazi; and the Chetniks really side with the Germans. Does it matter if it's true? . . . It's repeated and repeated, and it's very simply principled. . . ."

One evening in the urinal of a nightspot, Wut is recognized by some members of his former outfit and murdered as a traitor. His death is characteristically grotesque but presented with an edge of humor: he is stuffed head first into the chasm of a "crapper stall."

Vratno witnesses this, then escapes harm by claiming that he has just met Wut that evening. On the road, later, he meets up with an old Serb who criticizes King Peter's capitulation to Tito as the "best choice for Yugoslavia," and tells of a song the Serbs were singing, "We don't want Tito the bandit—we want the king, though he is no good!" When Vratno objects that they should not want the king, the old man replies, "Better a grave than a slave!"—to which Vratno replies, "Anything's better than a grub [grave]." From the old man Vratno gets a transit permit and a new identity, and as Siegfried Schmidt, he crosses into Austria on Wut's 1933 Grand Prix racer. He arrives in Vienna in 1945, about the time the Soviets begin "liberating" the city:

> The Soviets were supposed to be liberating the city, but for a liberating army they did a surprising amount of raping and such. The Soviets obviously had difficulty considering Austria as a real victim of Germany; they'd seen so many Austrian soldiers fighting with the Germans on the Russian front.

In thus reviewing the histories of Austria and Yugoslavia, Irving explores dramatically the concept of freedom that is in the heart of the novel. Like the animals, especially the bears in the zoo, his fictional characters' families are caught in a trap in which they are helpless. The two main historical moments of the narrative are different, though in certain respects they are related. The *Anschluss* was a planned and organized takeover, the planning and manipulation being handled behind the scenes—politicians were pressured and decisions were made for them. Schuschnigg was unable to resist Hitler; he felt that the Austrians and Germans were essentially one people. The people had no real say in the outcome; it was thrust upon them, and many happily acquiesced. The Yugoslavian situation, on the other hand, was chaotic, and Tito emerged the leader out of this chaos. Much of the internal warfare was tribal, the Ustashi becoming the most notorious, and had little relationship to the larger European situation. Even the acceptance of Tito, whose ancestry was both Serbian and Croatian, had its roots in tribal preferences.

The Yugoslavian upheaval was also much more violent than the Austrian collapse. Irving can comically undercut the events leading up to the *Anschluss* with a vision of a man in an eagle suit walking the streets of an Austrian town, but his descriptions of the Yugoslavian turmoil remain terrifying and hard-edged:

> My father would always remember a raft snagged in some deadfall along the bank. The raft was neatly piled with heads; the architect had attempted a pyramid. It was almost perfect. But one head near the peak had slipped out of place; its hair was caught between other heads, and it swung from face to face in the river wind; some faces watched the swinging, and some looked away.

Irving's language here is remarkable for its quiet tone—he seems able to contemplate the grotesque horrors of war with a matter-of-factness and acceptance that is unusual in American writing. Certainly, these images are not conducive to the existential ramifications commonly dealt in by protagonists who are coming of age in American war novels. Greil Marcus points out:

> For the American imagination . . . the burden of making sense of some of the central facts of our time has been slipped. That burden has been taken up, instead,

almost exclusively by writers from South America and, especially, eastern Europe, where those facts have been enforced so completely as to permanently alter the perception of what it means for a writer to depict ordinary life. For an American, it is precisely the eastern European writer's refusal to speak in a voice of shock, of distance, that is so shocking.[5]

Irving's characters walk through his fantastic landscape like animals suddenly released from a zoo, faced with an unreal situation that they are unable to control or even comprehend. The Marter family leaves Vienna and escapes to Kaprun, where they wait out the war, like many other helpless pawns in a political power struggle presided over by a maniac. Vratno Javotnik attempts to survive in the midst of chaos by playing all sides against the middle, to remain free by attaching himself to nothing. But, as ever in Irving's world, Vratno's freedom is only an illusion.

As is recounted in Siggy's diary, Vratno and Hilke Marter meet in Vienna in 1945, when Vratno and his motorcycle are found hiding in the Marters' old apartment upon the family's return. As Hilke soon discovers that she is pregnant, the two are married, coincidentally, on the last day of the Potsdam conference.

On the day Siggy is born, his grandmother is accidentally shot by a Russian patrolling the district. Irving depicts the Russian rule of this section of Vienna as a savage affair, punctuated by wild shootings, rapes, and bombings. Prominent in the sector is the Benno Blum gang, a black market group who for "the privilege of operating in the Russian sector . . . deftly did away with people. Benno Blum's Boys would waylay people all over Vienna, and skulk back to the Russian sector when the heat was on—although the Soviets claimed to be hunting down Benno Blum too." (This gang will figure prominently in Irving's third novel, *The 158-Pound Marriage.*)

In 1953, upon the death of Stalin, Vratno and Hilke go out to celebrate. In a restaurant, Vratno is confronted by Todor Slivinca, who managed to survive when Wut blew up his family's car. Vratno abruptly leaves with him and never returns. When Grandfather Marter later questions Slivinca as to Vratno's whereabouts, Todor points to some custard on the table and replies ominously, "Where is Vratno Javotnik? Why he's here, on your nose, and here, on the lantern overhead—and even here! in space."

In 1956, a year after the Soviets leave Vienna, Hilke abandons her family, who has moved back to Kaprun. That same year, during a snowfall, Grandfather Marter, in a last symbolic gesture, dresses up in the eagle suit, takes the mail sled, and hikes several miles toward the summit of the Kitzsteinhorn. He then rides the sled down the mountain, but is thrown off when it bangs into a log, and freezes to death. He is buried in the eagle suit by Siggy and Ernst Watzek-Trummer.

Although Irving's recounting of history, with its emphasis on repression, murder, and corruption, may sound like the distorted view of a nihilist, he does not share the "so it goes," "ho-hum," attitude of Kurt Vonnegut. (Unlike Vonnegut and some of his other absurdist contemporaries, Irving refuses to accept the inevitability of man's victimization—indeed, rebellion and defiance form one of the cornerstones of his vision, and his several protagonists here are the first in a series of defiant men.) Irving looks closely at the history of his age, because he believes that it must be known and assimilated. He shares the attitude of Watzek-Trummer, "supreme historian," who passes the lessons of history on to Siggy. In his epilogue

Siggy remarks that Ernst no longer reads as much as he used to and that he is often unimpressed with the books he is brought—"I know it already," he says.

John Irving, too, wants his readers to "know it," for remembering the horror of the past is essential in Irving's world. The characters in Irving's fiction who either know of the past or learn it become suspicious of life and are not surprised by it. In the notebook that Siggy keeps while planning the zoo break, he writes,

> At the risk of sounding polemical, I'd like to say that there are two ways to live a long time in this world. One is to trade with violence strictly as a free agent, with no cause or love that overlaps what's expedient; and if you give no direct answers, you'll never be discovered as lying to protect yourself. But I don't exactly know what the other way to live a long time is, although I believe it involves incredible luck.

The first part is not precisely true, as Vratno Javotnik's history demonstrates. For Irving, the second part is perhaps the only valid answer—luck.

Greil Marcus writes that "a rejection of euphemism and an insistence on remembering all that takes place"[4] makes resistance possible in Irving's universe. This is important, for if Irving accepts history, and to a certain extent he does, he refuses to submit to it. There is still room for the heroic gesture—Watzek-Trummer and Grandfather Marter's gestures, for example. They are like the Famous Asiatic Black Bears, who in the zoo must be enclosed by iron because they are "capable of digging through concrete." These bears, then, represent what is undeniable in man, the nonconformist attitude. Siggy's desire to set free the animals is an attempt to emulate

Zahn Glanz, whom he claims proudly as a relation, and who he feels was responsible for an unsuccessful zoo break twenty years before. Siggy feels that Austria has not learned enough from its history and needs to be awakened from its complacency—in his notebook he writes that the zookeeper, one O. Schrutt, is a sadistic ex-Nazi who tortures the animals. Siggy, however, does not live to carry out his protest; the last words Hannes records in Siggy's notebook are a statement Mihailovich made at his trial: "I wanted much . . . I started much . . . but the gale of the world blew away me and my world."

Although Hannes feels that Siggy, too, blew himself away, he decides to finish his friend's work and free the animals. He reasons that he has three choices: "The anticlimax, no climax at all, or the raging, unreasonable but definite climax demanded by the Famous Asiatic Black Bear." This is surely a reference to Yugoslavia, the Austrians, and the act of defiance that Irving feels is necessary: the Asiatic Black Bears are not like the Rare Spectacled Bears who, when Hannes opens their cages, were "hiding behind their drinking and dunking pool" and who have to be shouted at before they will come out from captivity.

The zoo break is a failure; most of the animals are rounded up and there are some casualties. When the incident is referred to again in *Garp*—this time recounted as the work of a woman—Irving writes,

> But the animals are well-fed and content now; only a few of them can even be goaded into leaving their cages, and those who do wander out are easily confined in the Schönbrunn paths and gardens; eventually they are returned to their cages, unharmed. One elderly bear suffers a bout of violent diarrhea. The old wom-

an's gesture of liberation is well intended, but it is completely meaningless and totally unrealized.

Hannes, too, feels that his gesture is, finally, meaningless and decides to go and discuss it with Watzek-Trummer, who "has had enough experience with pointless schemes to be sympathetic." His thoughts, in the meantime, are glum: "What worse awareness is there than to know there would have been a better outcome if you'd never done anything at all? That all small mammals would have been better off if you'd never meddled in the unsatisfactory scheme of things." However, while he is alone in the woods, contemplating what to do next, Hannes sees a pair of Rare Spectacled Bears ambling down the road. Hannes is thankful, "that their escape didn't take on the custard-like quality of too many other endings"; he is comforted by their escape, even if it is to be only temporary. Hannes has assimilated the lessons of history, and this ending suggests that his education will have positive effects. He has learned what life will have in store for him and about the finality of death.

*Setting Free the Bears* anticipates *Garp* in its preoccupation with death. Most of the central characters in the novel die; even Vratno's motto, "Better a slave than a grave," is meaningless, for Vratno, too, dies. The gesture, however, the need to assert oneself and one's responsibility, is essential, and at the end Hannes admits to "being responsible" for the casualties left behind at the zoo. His final thoughts are positive and look forward at least to an enlightened future. In the end he has become someone who can operate Siggy's motorcycle, one who is "properly balanced," steady, and doesn't panic, and who is ready to "outdrive the wind."

*Setting Free the Bears* has many flaws, primarily in its sketchy characterization and construction. Only

Siggy's Prehistory displays the power and novelistic scope that mark Irving as an exceptionally talented writer; it also contains the novel's thematic center. However, in its importance to an understanding of Irving's world, it is central. Prior to *Garp* it is his most important philosophical statement, dramatically detailing the European experience of World War II that is the central incident in shaping his vision. It will remain significant through his work, lurking in the background of his second and third novels, before its lessons are brilliantly crystallized in his masterpiece, *The World According to Garp*.

# CHAPTER 3

# Trumper's Complaint

In his first novel Irving portrayed two heroes "at loose ends," bent on reforming a static world in "an interim time." In *The Water-Method Man*, he concentrates instead on a single character, Fred "Bogus" Trumper, who is coming apart at the seams, concerned only with saving himself. Unlike *Setting Free the Bears*, which was essentially a meditation on history, this second novel is a story of spiritual and personal dislocation. Trumper's predicament is not conditioned by the overwhelming, impersonal forces of a world at war, but by his own confused feelings.

In some ways Fred Trumper is a nonintellectual Herzog—a bungler, a *schlemiel*, yet a humane and rather nice guy. Frequently blundering into mistakes and accidents, he correctly sees his existence as threatened by "little things—errors of judgment, but never crimes." Unlike Herzog, however, Trumper does not brood about history, philosophy, or politics, nor attempt to place his experience into any larger context; his aim is, simply, to survive. Indeed, Irving's hero has a problem that even poor Moses Herzog was spared: a birth defect has turned his urinary tract into "a narrow winding road." Unwilling to commit himself to surgery, he opts for "the water method," a treatment prescribed by a French urologist, requiring him to drink large quantities of water before and after sex to flush himself out.

The style of the novel reflects Trumper's dislocation, making this Irving's most intricately structured work, as his narrative moves backward and forward in time, varying between first-person, third-person, and epistolary modes, and even presenting some chapters in the form of a film script, which gently mocks Trumper's actions. Irving obviously had some fun with this, but it is a device he would afterwards abandon, as his next two novels again feature traditional, chronological plots, with only occasional interruptions in a progressive story line. Commenting on this novel, Irving said:

> When I went back to work on *The Water-Method Man*, I felt much more sophisticated—and I wanted to do everything. I wanted to write a book, if I could, with a happy ending, because I didn't feel I had a happy ending in me, and I wanted to get one. I wanted to write a book that was absolutely comic: I wanted it to be intricate and funny and clever and I wanted it to go on and on and on. I just blew it out.[1]

*The Water-Method Man* is indeed a "happy book," conspicuously lacking the corrosive bitterness of *Setting Free the Bears* and the extreme violence that is part of all his other work. It is a very warm and tender novel, a celebration of the human community and spirit and of man's capacity to endure. Irving has never been a nihilist, but Trumper is not even subjected to the kinds of setbacks, shocks, and losses that other Irving protagonists have to face. Unlike Garp or the figures in Siggy's historical narrative, Trumper's story is not potentially the stuff of tragedy, but has a rather slapstick, playful air about it.

The novel concentrates mostly on two periods in Trumper's life: his immediate past as a graduate student in comparative literature at the University of Iowa, including family life with his wife Sue "Biggie" Kunft and their son Colm, and his present circumstances in New York City, where he lives with a woman named Tulpen and works as a sound mixer for filmmaker Ralph Packer. The New York sections are narrated mostly in the first person—later in the novel it is revealed that Trumper is trying to write a diary in order to make sense of his experience. The diary's first line, "Her gynecologist recommended him to me," is also the first line of the novel; parts of the novel are thus to be taken as the completed diary of Fred Trumper. His past in Iowa and in Vienna with his friend Merrill Overturf are presented in the third person. The novel's structure is a kind of puzzle posed to the reader, an elaboration of Trumper's question, "How is everything related to anything else?" The enigma is compounded by Irving's relating to his protagonist's life the plot of the epic poem that Trumper is translating as his Ph.D. thesis.

The novel's construction dramatizes not only Trumper's dilemma but also the predicament of Irving's other characters, who suffer from an excess of self-knowledge while yet unable to extricate themselves from the various traps in which they find themselves. In an interview Irving suggested that his own creative effort involves an alternating perspective that perhaps reflects the personal duality evinced by his characters:

> Whenever I have written something for any length of time in the first person, I always want to get to the third

person, to get that distance again. And, whenever I
spend much time with the third person, I miss the first
person. They are very distinctive; they are very different voices. . . . That is exactly what *The Water-Method
Man* does. *The Water-Method Man* sort of takes the
liberty of using whatever voice it wants to for what will
suit the occasion.[2]

Trumper, in this connection, can see his past quite
objectively; it is the present he cannot deal with, for
here there are too many "little things" weighing him
down.

When first introduced, Fred Trumper is desperately searching for a "new life," while at the same time
he is appearing in a film about his life, appropriately
titled *Fucking Up*. When it is released, one critic's
synopsis of Trumper's life on film can also serve as a
description of his life off-camera:

Bogus Trumper, credited with the film's innovative
sound track, gives a fine acting performance in the role
of an aloof, tight-lipped failure with one busted marriage in his past, one cool and shaking relationship in
the present—an absolute paranoiac victimized by his
own self-analysis.

One of Trumper's central problems is his relationship
with Tulpen, the girlfriend to whom he is unable to
commit himself emotionally or legally. This inertia is
an extension of a general state of torpor and malaise
—Trumper can't seem to do anything. Tulpen tells
him, "you've got no direction, there's not a plan in
your life. There's no plot to it even." Later she
elaborates on this problem when she says, "No one
knows you, Trumper! You don't *convey* anything. You
don't do much, either. Things just sort of happen to
you. And they don't even add up to anything. You
don't make anything of what happens to you."

When Tulpen mentions wanting to have a baby,
Trumper simply sidesteps the issue—his customary
reaction. In one of the scenes from the film, Irving
crystallizes the relationship: ". . . Trumper and Tulpen are looking at a tangled mess of tape which has
spun off a reel and is spilling into a great wormy pile
on the floor. . . . Bogus Trumper, in stop-action, is
stooping to attempt to untangle a mess of spilled tape.
Tulpen is looking on." Trumper, at this stage, is
recovering from a near nervous collapse. He is struggling only to survive, a state he must pass beyond if he
is to become whole again. But, as the narrative of his
past reveals, even survival is a haphazard undertaking.

Trumper's troubles are shown to have begun
with his marriage to Biggie, an American skier whom
he meets in Austria. When Biggie gets pregnant, the
newlyweds must face Trumper's straight-laced parents upon their return to America. Dr. Trumper, a
humorless and conservative man who expected his
son to finish his education before marrying, promptly
disinherits him, leaving Trumper to try to make ends
meet as a graduate assistant in Iowa City with a wife
and a baby.

Financial problems soon overwhelm him. Biggie
returns to her old job at the hospital, "bedpanning
the elderly between 6 A.M. and noon," and Trumper
takes on a weekend job of selling pennants and
souvenirs at Iowa football games. None of this helps
very much, and the debts mount. Meanwhile, Trumper is working halfheartedly on his Ph.D. thesis, a
translation of the Old Low Norse epic *Akthelt and
Gunnel,* which is to include "a sort of etymological
dictionary of Old Low Norse." This, too, is giving
Trumper headaches, although his father unhelpfully
reminds him, "with your Ph.D. you'll have a profes-

sion that's dependable. But every professional man must suffer his training."

Irving's parody of academe provides some of the most amusing sections of the novel. In describing the reaction of Dr. Holster (Trumper's thesis adviser) to his proposed topic, Irving writes:

> Dr. Holster was very interested in such a dictionary; he felt it would be of some etymological use. That was why he approved the thesis topic; he actually thought *Akthelt and Gunnel* was junk, though he was hard-pressed to prove it. Dr. Holster didn't know any Old Low Norse at all.

Therefore, when Trumper has difficulty with the dictionary, he can solve it readily enough:

> Since no one knew anything about Old Low Norse, I could make things up. I made up a lot of origins. This made the translation of *Akthelt and Gunnel* easier too. I started making up a lot of words. It's very hard to tell real Old Low Norse from made-up Old Low Norse.
> Dr. Wolfram Holster never knew the difference.

During the course of the novel, however, Trumper himself begins to identify with the narrative and to echo some of its philosophy. One stanza he translates to read: "Gunnel loved to look at Akthelt/ His knife was so long./ But she knew in her heart/ The world was too strong." Trumper writes that both Dr. Holster and Biggie laughed at that stanza, but he cannot. The overpowering pressure of external reality is central to Irving's fiction, and the sense of it traumatizes his protagonists, especially such sensitive ones as Trumper and Garp, who react to the world by trying to withdraw from it, desperately attempting to shelter their children from any exposure to pain or suffering. (The attempts of Trumper and Garp to protect their children and to remain sane amid the constant intrusions of an irrational world provide some of Irving's most compassionate moments, making those characters easily, totally sympathetic.) Trumper feels that "the author was trying to foreshadow the inevitable doom! Clearly Akthelt and Gunnel were headed for grief. I knew and I simply didn't want to see it out." Trumper must learn to confront grief and to live with the knowledge of it—this is one of the primary lessons of Siggy's journal, and in writing his own diary, Trumper will learn to cope with these things himself.

Another passage that greatly affects Trumper is from a section of the poem detailing Akthelt's attempt to explain to Gunnel the object of war, to which she refuses to listen. Old Thak, Akthelt's father, a kindly, generous man (a clear foil to Trumper's own father) asserts that "the object of war is to survive it." Trumper adds, "Which struck me as the object of graduate school—and possibly my marriage. Such comparisons struck me hard in those days." As Irving's novels make clear, survival in itself is something of an accomplishment, although Siggy's journal certainly demonstrates that it is not enough, and this, too, Fred Trumper will learn.

The *Akthelt and Gunnel* episodes gradually become significant in another light, for in addition to counterpointing Trumper's predicament, they also digress in tenor from his situation and its outcome. Trumper's story is presented in a lighthearted way, with even a happy ending, whereas *Akthelt and Gunnel* is closer to the stark, violent world of Siggy's Prehistory, a world of war and death and destruction. There is, first, the gruesome murder of Old Thak, Akthelt's father, who, betrayed by a member of his tribe, is riddled with arrows aboard his ship. In a later sequence, Sprog, Akthelt's servant, thinking that his master wants to change wives (a partial anticipation of *The 158-Pound Marriage*), attempts to have sex with Gunnel, for which he is "de-balled with a battle-ax"— Trumper's own problems with the water method are mild in comparison with the fate of poor Sprog, and his sufferings for his indiscretions are not nearly so final.

The ending of the poem is especially horrible: Akthelt returns home one day to discover that Hrothrund, the murderer of his father, has attempted to abduct Gunnel. As Akthelt thereafter begins to believe that Gunnel was unfaithful to him, she sets out to capture Hrothrund in order to prove her innocence. However, fearing a plot against him, Akthelt sets his wife's ship afloat and it is captured by Hrothrund. Gunnel then feigns love for her captor and offers herself to him:

> For days and nights in his foul ship's cabin hung with animal skins, Gunnel gave up her body to his savage, slimy ways, until at last he fully trusted her. He would take her, unarmed, without his knife or broad-ax by his bedside, and rut like a contented beast, leaving her gasping. He was fool enough to think it was pleasure that made her gasp.

One day she decapitates Hrothrund and stuffs his head with live eels. Then she returns to Akthelt, who begs her forgiveness, but soon afterwards she decapitates her husband as well and goes mad. The tribal warfare that follows parallels the Yugoslav's history in *Setting Free the Bears:* "Finally, when the kingdom of Thak was hardly even a kingdom any more, but a disorganized land with hundreds of tiny, feuding fiefs, what happened then was what *always* happens

too." Young Axelrulf takes over the warring kingdom
—"He made peace in the kingdom by killing all the
feuders who wanted war." Also, he marries, and in
the last stanza of the poem, the author concludes that
"the story of Axelrulf and Gronigen is probably not
much different from the story of Akthelt and Gunnel.
So why not stop it here?"

This violent tale always lurks in the background
of Trumper's own experience, balancing the gentler
vision of the main narrative and suggesting that while
Trumper is at last given a second chance, this happens very rarely: witness the fate of poor Akthelt. It
also emphasizes the insular nature of Trumper's
story, shading it with the harsher realities of a larger
world—in *Akthelt and Gunnel,* as in *Setting Free the
Bears,* almost everyone dies a violent death.

Trumper's marriage, finances, and thesis are not
his only problems: Lydia Kindle, a student, is in love
with him, and he lusts after her but is indecisive (as
usual) over what to do about it. She takes matters into
her own hands when she picks him up in a parking
lot, drives him out into the deserted countryside,
undresses, and offers herself to him. Then Trumper
realizes that he can't go through with it; as he slips on
a condom—"I hear the tin foil tear and crinkle: I
wonder if she hears it too"—and begins making love
to her, he suddenly thinks about "slaughterhouses
and . . . all those young girls raped in war." At this
point he decides against consummating their relationship and gets out of the car. Outraged, Lydia throws
his clothes out of the car and leaves Trumper, naked,
save for a rubber, standing on the "duck-flown shores
of the Coraville reservoir!"

Trumper, then, must atone for even thinking of
infidelity—in Irving's universe both fidelity and infidelity seem impossible—and he walks and jogs bare-
foot through watery fields until he gets a ride from

two men returning from duck hunting. By this time his feet are swollen and bloody and he is physically exhausted. In a mock ritual of penance, Trumper is asked to hold one of the ducks:

> . . . I gingerly took it by its rubbery neck. . . . Only the wing tips and the head were still feathered: a lovely wood duck with a multicolored face. There weren't more than three or four pellet wounds in it; the ugliest wound was the naked slit where it had been dressed out. His great feet felt like armchair leather. And there was a dried, see-through bead of blood, like small dull marble, on the tip of his beak.

Dropping him off in town, the hunters give Trumper the duck, which he takes home with him. Next, in trying to sneak in through the basement, he asserts his *schlemiel*-hood and further aggravates his foot when he steps on a mousetrap and catches his toe: "I couldn't stop the scream, because I didn't realize what I'd stepped on until it was at a crescendo." Trumper then further complicates the situation when he lies to Biggie, explaining that he has been duck hunting. He is unmasked when he pulls down his fly at the toilet and without realizing it, urinates into his rubber. Biggie is incensed, and screams at him, while Trumper hysterically asks for a scissors. While all this is going on, the mailman walks in with a special-delivery letter.

This incident is revealing, for it effectively summarizes Irving's attitudes and his treatment of theme and character in this novel. Even though Trumper pays for his impulse toward infidelity, the whole sequence is handled in an indulgent, comic way—the reader must sympathize with Trumper. He is a clown, a bungler, yet loving and decent, all of which is demonstrated in his desire for Lydia and his inability to consummate it, his encounter with the mousetrap, and his forgetting to remove the condom.

The predominance of blood in the sequence, however, links it with other violent and tragic confrontations in the other novels: Siggy is stung to death; in *The 158-Pound Marriage,* children are cut and wounded in a bath, in a sense punished for their parents' infidelities; Garp and Helen, too, are punished for infidelity when one son dies and the other loses an eye in an automobile accident. Garp, indeed, is able to work out his pain and guilt in a novel, *The World According to Bensenhaver,* which contains an episode similar in detail to Trumper's—two people isolated in a countryside setting, the concentration on blood and sex in an automobile, and the condom as a significant object in the drama. In *Garp,* the scene is violent and grotesque, involving murder and rape; here, on the other hand, Irving's attitude toward his character is distinctly playful—it seems he lacks the distance that he will bring to *Garp* (and which Garp himself does not have). Trumper, less eccentric than this successor and largely presented through first-person narrative, is a more readily sympathetic figure, and consequently his story is less accessible to the kinds of violence that Irving describes in the other books. In *The Water-Method Man*—Irving's only novel that does not have a central violent episode—most of the blood comes not from mutilated human beings, but, appropriately, from the dead duck. (Indeed, the novel's only real violence occurs in the poem *Akthelt and Gunnel,* which depicts rape and decapitation, but it is here sufficiently distanced by its inclusion as a fiction within a fiction and by the saga's overtly barbaric medieval setting. Nevertheless, these lurid scenes demonstrate, as the *Bensenhaver* episode will in the later novel, how effectively Irving can portray violence and brutality.)

Trumper is now at his lowest point. He recalls another sequence from *Akthelt and Gunnel*, in which Akthelt wants to take his son, Axelrulf, with him on a campaign against some enemies, the Greths. His wife, however, will not allow it, fearing the boy will see his father "take a woman"—again, it is the prospect of infidelity rather than any physical danger which causes the trouble. Trumper, however, writes that the episode is significant because, in the end, "Akthelt left Axelrulf at home with his mother; he did it Gunnel's way after all." Biggie, too, gets Colm, upon their separation, and Trumper is left alone.

The special-delivery letter, containing a five-thousand-dollar loan from his father, gives Trumper a reprieve—he pays all of his debts, buys a plane ticket for Vienna, and leaves the balance of money for Biggie. Vienna is a special place for Trumper, the locale of a youthful jaunt and a ski trip with his best friend Merrill Overturf, as well as the scene of his meeting and marrying Biggie. Beginning with *The Water-Method Man,* this city regularly functions as a formative place for Irving's American characters, as well as a haven in times of stress.

Merrill is remembered as a wild, anarchic personality who, because of a bad diabetic problem, had adopted a devil-may-care attitude to life: he was adventurous, unpredictable, and completely zany. Trumper loved him, and when they lived together in Vienna, took care of him, gave him insulin, and monitored his sugar count. Still, Trumper thinks of Merrill as "the great illusion of my life. That such a self-destroying fool could be so indestructible." Later, admitting that he and Biggie hardly saw Merrill in Vienna, he explains, "we were too vulnerable to his humor; he made us aware how our casualness was faked." Merrill is the wayward, romantic extension of Trumper's own personality, that part of him which inspires him to some daring or imaginative act and then naturally leads to a pratfall. The connection is emphasized by Merrill's interest in the Vienna zoo break which links him with Siggy, Hannes's romantic extension, whose death also paves the way for Hannes's liberation.

Trumper's current European experience is bizarre, and he seems to wander through it as if in a fog. When he arrives, he buys a typewriter on which to keep a journal, acquires a romantic-looking costume that makes him resemble "a travelling spy who had been a passenger on the Orient Express," and checks into a pension which also functions as a whorehouse. He never finds Merrill, but does manage to become involved in an adventure with the Secret Service when he accidently gets hold of some hashish. All through this Trumper is never himself; his "mind is lost." Having helped the Secret Service to apprehend the pusher, he receives a free trip back to the United States. From a Secret Service agent, he learns that Merrill is dead—his hero-image is gone. Earlier Irving has written, "Bogus' longest dreams are about heroes. Accordingly, he dreams of Merrill Overturf, sterilizing his hypodermic needle and syringe in a little saucepan, and boiling a test tube of Benedict's solution and pee to check his urine sugar." At last he comes to an understanding of what he subconsciously felt when he arrived in Vienna: "that adventure is a time and not a place."

His friend gone and his illusions crushed, Trumper decides to put his life in order, and this resolve is reinforced when he learns that during his absence Biggie has remarried and is living in Maine. Her new husband, Couth, is another childhood friend much admired by Trumper, for he is at peace with himself and lives as he wants to, free of the kinds of traumas and troubles that plague Trumper. Determining to free himself as well, Trumper now makes a gesture that is both practical and symbolic of his new active approach toward the tangled mess of his life: at last dissatisfied with the water method, he undergoes an operation that solves his urinary problem. Having overcome this physical ailment, emblematic of the troubled life that needs to be flushed clean, he is ready to tackle his emotional and spiritual problems as well.

One of Trumper's first decisions after his surgery is to finish his thesis: "All he knew was that he had never finished anything, and he felt a need, almost as basic as survival, to find something he could finish." Again, his attitude is affected by the tale of Akthelt and Gunnel, specifically by the episode in which Old Thak, Akthelt's father, is killed: "Akthelt smears his body with the blood of his father, orders himself lashed to the mainmast and commands his men to whip him with the shafts of the fatal arrows until his own blood runs with his father's." This image, the merging of the father and the son, persuades Trumper of the need to assume responsibility—something with which his own father is obsessed—and the necessary obligations of life. He starts his thesis again from the beginning, producing a complete translation and glossary. It is a scholarly and thorough job this time; nothing is made up.

In addition to completing his thesis, Trumper moves back in with Tulpen, who, during his absence, has borne his child, named Merrill. He decides to commit himself seriously to this new family relationship; he also starts looking for a teaching job and reconciles himself with his parents. Meanwhile, the film *Fucking Up* is released and receives rave reviews, which makes Trumper something of a celebrity.

The novel concludes in Maine, where Tulpen, Trumper, Biggie, Couth, and Ralph Packer and his new bride, Matje, all gather to observe Throgsgafen Day, an orgiastic holiday orginating in the kingdom of Thak. Here Trumper is reunited with all the people he loves in an ecstatic celebration of love and friendship:

> ". . . it occurred to him that he was actually at peace with himself for the first time in his life. He realized how much he'd been anticipating peace someday, but the feeling was not what he'd expected. He used to think that peace was a state he would achieve, but the peace he was feeling was like a force he'd submitted to."

One of the stories that Trumper is most fond of telling Colm is of Moby Dick: "Colm thought whales were wonderful, so the story according to Trumper was the whale as hero, Moby Dick as unvanquished king." This is how Trumper sees himself at the end of the novel—a symbol of unvanquished endurance, but more important than that, "someone who is mindful of his scars, his old harpoons and things," but who also realizes the necessity of love, commitment, and "all the good flesh around him."

In *The Water-Method Man,* Irving manages with great success to assemble the disparate fragments of a man's life into a moving, rich, and satisfying whole. He introduces here, in sharp focus, the themes and subjects that will preoccupy him in the subsequent fiction: the wisdom of distrusting "facts" and the need to look beyond them, marriage and the impossibility yet necessity of fidelity, the vulnerability of children, the overwhelming strength of the physical world, and the emotional nature of violence. The form of the novel, in certain ways like *Setting Free the Bears* and like the novels to follow, demonstrates dramatically Irving's basic sympathy with his protagonist's need to make sense out of experience and his contention that the only way to do that is through art (writing). Thus, Irving's works, which employ structure as a means of talking about structure, argue implicitly that art is one of the only means of salvation in a world that is too strong to be confronted haphazardly or half-heartedly. In *The Water-Method Man*, more than in any of the other novels, Irving manages to convey both the mystery and the wonder of that difficult life— here he succeeds, in one critic's words, in making "from the *dreck* of daily lives . . . the improbable seem likely"—and, in the process, "retrieves something of beauty."[3]

# CHAPTER 4

# The Good Wrestler

*The 158-Pound Marriage* is Irving's most corrosive work, and also his most self-consciously literary one, exhibiting a marked departure from *The Water-Method Man* in its treatment of character and in its tone. Once again, he examines the ways that people have of destroying each other, although this time, the marriage relationship is given almost exclusive focus—we are outside the realm of history invoked in *Setting Free the Bears* and that of the individual crisis which was the primary concern of *The Water-Method Man*. In this work, the saga of Akthelt and Gunnel is given contemporary treatment, with a less violent though still brutal outcome.

Irving's third novel remains linked to his others in its overt concern with novelistic form and design; however, Irving abandons here the multiple narrative technique to present the entire novel in the first person. His narrator juggles with chronology, manipulating his audience by holding back some essential information during certain sequences and filling it in later. The form is, nevertheless, basically chronological, although this tendency does necessitate occasional abrupt transitions from the present into the past.

This novel also continues to deal with places, motifs, and themes common to the earliest works: Vienna, the male protagonist's protective obsession with his children, the aloof father figure; fidelity/infidelity; and sudden, shattering violence.

Irving's comments on the origins of this novel are revealing:

> I got this idea for a literary novel: given the company I was keeping—and I mean the books I was reading, too—that was understandable. *The 158-Pound Marriage* is about two couples—a sexual foursome—and it grew very specifically out of Ford Madox Ford's *The Good Soldier* and John Hawkes' *The Blood Oranges*. If I'd not read those two books, I would not have written *The 158-Pound Marriage*. That's the kind of period I was in at the time: everything I read was a *labor* and it made me *angry*. It was like I lost my sense of humor.[1]

This novel is indeed deeply indebted to both Ford and Hawkes; Irving even quotes a passage from each novel as a double epigraph (a device he has not used before or since). All three novels share a basic plot structure, involving the interrelationship of two married couples, although Irving's book is perhaps closer to Hawkes's in its almost exclusive focus on the couples and their decision to swap mates. (Ford's novel concentrates on a love triangle, with a fifth party actually being more involved in the novel's action than one of the couples.) Briefly, *The 158-Pound Marriage* revolves around two international couples: the narrator, an American historical novelist, finds himself attracted to an American woman who has hopes of becoming a writer, whereas her husband, a professor of German (employed at the same university as the narrator) and wrestling coach, finds in the narrator's wife another Viennese victim of World War II. The novel explores the past lives of these characters prior to their marriages and the history of the sexual experiment that they undertake.

The three novels are all narrated in the first person by a central male participant in the action, and Irving combines in his work aspects of both of the earlier narrators' functions. In Ford's *The Good Soldier,* Dowell's narrative is, in part, an attempt to piece together what he calls "the saddest story I have ever heard" and so come to an understanding of it. This has always been one reason for Irving's use of first-person narrative, providing his characters the opportunity to review their lives and to place them in some kind of perspective—Siggy's journal is a first-person account (though here history is the subject to be sorted out), as is Fred Trumper's review of his past life. Irving's (nameless) narrator in this novel also seeks to comprehend both the nature of the complex relationship in which he has become involved and his own part in it. Yet this narrator wants more than simple understanding, and in this respect he is nearly related to Cyril, the "sex singer" and narrator of Hawkes's *The Blood Oranges,* for both characters endeavor also to justify their actions and behavior in the dramas they are describing. Both characters try, through their narratives, to slant their tales to their own advantage (as Dowell does not). Hawkes's narrator, however, "spins his tapestry" in an attempt to win back Catherine, his partner in the game of love, whereas Irving's narrator has no such desire—his narrative is merely an attempt to assimilate the experience and thus to justify himself.

*The Blood Oranges* and *The 158-Pound Marriage* are further likened by the two central male characters, Hugh in Hawkes's novel and Severin Winter in Irving's, whose essential distrust of the love experiments they enter upon injects notes of fatality and doom into the enterprises, and who play significant roles in the destruction of their respective affairs. In both novels the narrators fail to understand or come to grips with these antagonists; their narratives, in part, attempt to discredit them.

The makeup of Irving's two couples is interesting in its relationship to the two couples in *The Good Soldier*. Irving's couples, as mentioned earlier, are both international; during the course of the novel, the two Americans come together, as do the two Austrians. Ford, on the other hand, pits an English couple against an American couple, not involving them in an exchange of mates, though Florence Dowell (the narrator's wife) is for a time the mistress of Edward Ashburnham, the novel's central protagonist. Dowell himself enjoys no illicit sexual favors. The interesting link is in the novelists' attitudes about Americans and Europeans: both identify a vast cultural chasm between the experiences and the sensibilities common to natives of the two worlds. Ford's Americans are rootless and shallow—Dowell, himself an American, exposes his countrymen's endemic vulgarity when he tells of his wife's uncle, who took with him on a world's tour thousands of California oranges to give as presents to strangers:

> Four, to every person on board the several steamers that they employed, to every person with whom he had so much as a nodding acquaintance, he gave an orange every morning. And they lasted him right round the girdle of this mighty globe of ours. When they were at North Cape, even, he saw on the horizon, poor thin man that he was, a lighthouse. "Hello," says he to himself, "these fellows must be very lonely. Let's take them some oranges." So he had a boatload of his fruit out and had himself rowed to the lighthouse on the horizon.[2]

The Americans in Ford's novel seem unable to penetrate beneath life's surfaces, and their actions are thus either absurd or, in the case of Florence Dowell, selfish and evil. Irving, too, creates American characters who seem inadequate beside the Europeans. Severin Winter and Utch (the narrator's wife) have been tempered by their experiences as victims of war, which have given them a depth of understanding that the narrator and Edith (Severin's wife) cannot match. The Americans, here as well, are selfish, thoroughly carnal, and unable, as the narration makes very clear, to deal with complexities of feeling and thought.

Irving's novel breaks with its predecessors, however, in matters of tone and theme, and though enriched by the associations, it stands up very well on its own. *The Good Soldier* is a "sad story" that flirts with tragedy but does not achieve it; Ford's protagonists, Edward Ashburnham and Nancy Rufford, withdraw by suicide and insanity (respectively) from a world which they perceive as horrible. The background of Ford's novel, published in 1915, is pervaded by ominous tensions of the approaching World War, a cataclysm that ushered in the modern world, crushing in the process the traditional values of a simpler age. The suffering that Ford's characters endure is reflective of this external calamity; in a world bereft of meaning, the gestures of these figures have a dire absurdity about them.

Hawkes' smilieu, conversely, is one of the imagination, for his characters inhabit not a realistic locale —although in *The Blood Oranges*, Illyria is given just enough verisimilitude to veil its metaphoric nature— but a world created of words and art. Cyril, the narrator, finds in his imagination, the medium of his "word weavings," a haven, a point of stability, a refuge: "in Illyria there are no seasons." What takes place in this timeless setting, brought into being by an artist, is a confrontation of life forces—Eros, personified primarily by Cyril, and Thanatos, personified by Hugh. In an interview, Hawkes remarked that "I wanted to create characters in total purity and to deny myself the novelistic easiness of past lives to draw on,"[3] and his characters do exhibit a kind of metaphoric purity, as they confront each other as elementary opposites in a dialectic of life and death, time and timelessness. This statement also points up the major difference between Hawkes's narrator and Ford's—the former is an artist, the latter a diarist.[4]

*The 158-Pound Marriage*, however, is a comic tale about freedom and responsibility, in which the narrator himself learns nothing. Unlike Ford, Irving is not writing about the decline of one order and its replacement by an empty, immoral one, for his universe is one in which the givens are spiritual and moral emptiness, chaos, and violence. He takes for granted, albeit sadly, that man is in a state beyond redemption and that such concepts as faith and ideology, which may have once governed the world, are no longer viable—are, indeed, absent. Irving's European experience and his study of history no doubt fed and elaborated his own basic sense of the all-consuming power of atrocity. Irving's novel is thus, as much as Ford's, manifestly a product of its time: World War I cannot be dissociated from *The Good Soldier*, and *The 158-Pound Marriage* cannot be considered apart from the 1960s, the time frame of its major action and the sphere of its moral climate.

Irving's characters inhabit a grotesque black-comic universe, where a spirit of anarchy prevails and no moral or spiritual values remain to stabilize their lives. To some extent Irving shares the view of the modern French dramatists of the absurd, who believe, in Martin Esslin's words, that "the dignity of man lies in his ability to face reality in all its senselessness; to accept it freely, without fear, without illusions —and to laugh at it."[5] *The 158-Pound Marriage* presents a Dionysian world of almost unrestrained freedom in which human passions—"natural" agents far more terrifying than bears—have been set free. Irving's own judgment of this world is implied in the transparent selfishness of his narrator, certainly the most amoral central character in all of his fiction: a historical novelist who has learned nothing from history.

Unlike Hawkes, Irving requires that his drama be played out in the real world. Committed to the aesthetic values of verisimilitude and mimesis, and to the tenets of traditional plot construction and characterization, Irving has no use for imaginary settings, nor for "pure," archetypal characters—his people have detailed pasts, and history directly affects their lives. Time here is not the abstract concept vaguely perceptible in Hawkes's world, but a very specific and almost tangible force. Whereas Cyril in *The Blood Oranges* seeks to sidestep time, to avoid it as his one true enemy, Irving's characters are always preoccupied with it, recognizing a reality too important to ignore. Rather than attempting to deny the passage and effects of time, as Hawkes's narrator does, Irving's characters actually construct their fictions in order to substantiate it. For Irving, as it were, the narrator remarks, "Novels which did not convey real time conveyed nothing."

If Bogus Trumper is a portrait of someone who manages, finally, to accommodate that part of himself which craves freedom to an overriding sense of the limitations of freedom and of the need for personal responsibility and commitment, the narrator of Irving's third novel represents the opposite reaction. He even recognizes some of his own inadequacies, pinpointing his major problem when he writes: "You can tell a lot about someone by how he deals with insomnia. My reaction—to insomnia and to life in general—is to give in. My best-trained senses are passive; my favorite word is *yield*." In some ways he is like the Rare Spectacled Bears, "passively sad but accepting anything."

More important, however, is that, although he is a historical novelist, he has no perspective. Early in the narrative he correctly points out, "History takes time; I resist writing about people who are still alive". Yet he does just that in the story that unfolds. A second comment is even more ironic, in light of his performance here: "For history you need a camera with two lenses—the telephoto and the kind of close-up with a fine, penetrating focus. You can forget the wide-angle lens; there is no angle wide enough." All of Irving's novels demonstrate the falsity of that statement, as does the narrator's own narrative in this one. The "wide-angle lens" may not, indeed, be wide enough, but it is the business, the fundamental responsibility, of real historians—and Irving insists that all serious thinkers are such—to attempt a broad perspective; any true understanding must be "wide-angled." The narrator, unfortunately, inclines to the more limited focus, interpreting his story only from the "close-up" range, and he is so obsessed by his experiences that it colors his response to even the most unrelated phenomena. Musing about the wartime decapitation of the carved stone figure of an angel on the facade of the cathedral at Reims, he writes,

It's commonly said in that part of France that the moral of "The Smile of Reims" is that when there's a war on, and you're in it, don't be happy; you insult both the enemy and your allies. But the moral of "The Smile of Reims" isn't very convincing. The good people of Reims haven't got eyes for detail like mine. When the angel has her smile and head intact, the saint beside her is in pain. When her smile and the rest of her head leave her, that saint—despite new wounds of his own— seems more content. The moral of "The Smile of Reims" according to *me*, is that an unhappy man cannot tolerate a happy woman.

Such myopic exegesis—amusing as it may be—is indicative of the view the narrator takes of everything in the novel, his interpretation of events continually skewed by the anger and bitterness of his own involvement and by a fundamental lack of comprehension. Although his narrative continually implies that all essential information has been included, the faultiness of his perceptions makes of his tale-telling a complex and possibly deceptive business.

This narrator very much resembles Hawkes's Cyril in appearance: he is tall and thin, has a beard, and describes himself as "a woman's man." Most important, like Cyril, he is unable to come to grips with his own shortcomings. At one point, Cyril claims that "it is hardly a fault to have lived my life, and still to live it, without knowing pain"[6]; pain, death, and darkness are embodied in Hugh, in whose "dry mouth our lovely song became a shriek." Similarly, Irving's narrator's main antagonist, Severin Winter, is described as dark (as is Hugh), and one who "could pervert the most frankly innocent erotic things."

Severin Winter's history, like that of each of the other central characters, is detailed by the narrator in a chapter headed "Scouting Reports." Severin's roots are in Vienna, and the descriptions of his parents echo *Setting Free the Bears:* his mother was the actress Katrina Marek—it was under a poster bearing her

likeness that Zahn Glanz abandoned his cab—and his
father, Kurt Winter, was a minor expressionist painter who managed to get his pregnant wife out of
Austria on the day before the *Anschluss*. Severin then
grew up fatherless, never really knowing the fate of
his lost parent—he is one of three Irving protagonists
to grow up without a father (the others are Siggy and
Garp). Trumper and the narrator of this novel both
have cold, distant fathers, and the narrator's father
will die at the end of the novel. Severin speculates
that his father, who was full of revolutionary fervor,
drove the radical editor Lennhoff to Hungary—Zahn
Glanz, too, was credited with this feat—and that
twelve days before the Soviets captured Vienna, let
the animals out of the zoo. He remarks, "My father
loved animals and was just the right sort of sport for
the job. A devout antifascist, it must have been his last
act for the underground." This link makes Severin
Winter part of a gallery in Irving's world who are
intimately acquainted with the essential need for
freedom, though Severin stands out as one who
understands its implications and limitations. He combines the qualities of Siggy's romanticism—he is also
linked to Merrill Overturf in that he once drove a
Zorn-Witwer automobile—and the tempered understanding which Graff and Bogus Trumper acquire.
Severin is an older man; he is also a father whose
romanticism has been assimilated in a positive way—
children always force Irving's protagonists to attempt
some control over their lives.

     Severin was raised by his mother, first in London,
where he was born, and then in Vienna; she became
an artist's model and the subject of many erotic
paintings, many of which hang in Severin's bedroom.
After his mother's death, Severin was befriended by
two Chetnik freedom-fighters who had fled Tito and
who were also Olympic wrestlers. They encouraged

Severin to go to college in America, where he attended the University of Iowa, majoring in languages and
wrestling. As a wrestler, he was once a runner-up in
the middleweight class of the Big Ten Champion-
ships; wrestling remains for him a central metaphor
for life, and one that recurs repeatedly in the novel,
as the narrator regularly cites his terminology.

Returning from America, Severin resettled in
Vienna, and there met his wife Edith, the daughter of
wealthy New Yorkers, who was traveling in Europe
and hoping to become a writer. Requested by her
mother to find some minor modern European paintings for a museum's collection, Edith went to Vienna
to look up Severin Winter, the custodian of his
father's art collection. Anxious to sell some paintings
to raise money to leave Europe—"Everyone and
everything is dying here."—and go back to America,
Severin became her guide. Soon they fell in love, and
then married and honeymooned energetically in
Greece: "They made love in the morning, sometimes
twice, before getting up. They went to bed soon after
the evening meal, and if making love made them too
wide awake, which it often did, they would get up, go
out again and eat another supper. Then they'd make
love again." This youthful Severin is clearly a passionate and active young man—Edith once describes
him as a "baby bear"—but he is not the same man
whose personality dominates the novel's present action.

Closely linked to Severin, both in the experiences
of her past and in her basic attitude toward the
*ménage à quatre*, is the narrator's wife, Utch. Like
Severin, she was born in 1938, the year of the
*Anschluss;* at the age of three, she, too, lost her
father—also thought to be a revolutionary, he was
executed as a Bolshevik saboteur—and was raised by

her mother. Her early childhood was shadowed by
war, punctuated by the necessity of seeking shelter
from the Allied bombings of a munitions plant nearby her home.

When the Russians invaded Austria in 1945,
Utch, in her husband's words, "learned patience."
Aware that the occupying troops were looting the
country and raping its women, Utch's mother devised
an ingenious plan to protect her daughter:

> Going over to the largest cow, whose head was locked
> in its milking hitch, she slit the cow's throat. When it
> was dead, she unfastened the head from the milking
> hitch and rolled the cow on her side. She cut open the
> belly of the cow, pulled out the intestines and carved
> out the anus, and then made Utch lie down in the cavity
> between the great cow's ribs. . . . She closed the slit
> belly-flaps of the cow around Utch like a curtain; she
> told Utch she could breathe through the cow's carved-
> out anus.

Utch stayed inside the cow's belly—it seems a grotesque variation on Anne Frank's hiding place—until
she was discovered by a benevolent Russian soldier,
Captain Kudashvili. Shortly after her rescue, she
learned that her mother had been raped and killed.

Thereafter, Utch grew up in a Russian sector of
Vienna, protected by Kudashvili and by members of
the Benno Blum gang—the "most notorious criminal
gang in Vienna . . . responsible for the 'disappear-
ance' of that famous one-third of the anti-Soviets in
Vienna"—until the Russians departed in 1955. When
Kudashvili was killed during the Hungarian uprising
against the Russians a year later, Utch was left or-
phaned again. She remained in Vienna, studied languages (including English), and found translating
work. She met her husband, the narrator, while she

was conducting English tours in the Kunsthistorisches
Museum—like Edith, the narrator married his tour
guide.

About his own past the narrator tells very little.
His father, a history professor at Harvard for thirty-
six years, is distant, and his son calls him "sir." He
does not seem to take any real interest in his son's
career; his mother, however, is a fan of her son's
books. (The narrator writes that "as a rule, mothers
are more serious than fathers," and this holds true in
Irving's universe, although the children of these
"absent" or dead fathers generally become obsessive
parents themselves—the narrator is an exception.) In
1963, the narrator received a Ph.D. and decided to
write a novel based on Bruegel's painting *The Fight
Between Carnival and Lent*. Traveling to Vienna to
see the painting, he met Utch.

These four characters come together at a New
England university, where the narrator and Severin
are professors. They all meet one night at a dinner
party and thereafter develop the bizarre mate-
swapping relationship that changes their lives and
provokes the narrator's attempt to account for the
experience.

The central conflict in the story is between the
two men; the narrator blames Severin for the eventu-
al deterioration of the double affair because Severin
exhibits a dimension of severity and conservatism
that proves ultimately destructive to the relationship.
The dichotomy between Severin and the narrator is
best epitomized in Bruegel's painting, a copy of which
hangs in the narrator's kitchen: Carnival's representative is pictured riding on a wine barrel and brandish-
ing a spit with a pig on it in the direction of Lent, who
is thin and drawn and is warding off Carnival with a
shovel on which are two herrings. In the painter's

characteristic detailing, Carnival is surrounded by revelers indulging themselves in eating, lovemaking, and theatrical performances, whereas good deeds, such as almsgiving, praying, and burying the dead, are performed around Lent. Predictably, the narrator's description of the painting emphasizes the Carnival details, and he sees himself as the rich burgher figure in the right-hand corner: "I am moving from the church toward the inn; this seems wise." Bruegel's painting is more balanced: clearly virtue is on the side of Lent, but the outcome is still undecided. Many of the figures on the Lent side of the painting are not sympathetically drawn, and there is a balance to the composition that seems to suspend judgment. Most important, prominent in the center of the painting is a couple, viewed from behind, being led off by a fool. Where are they going? What does this mean? Irving's narrator does not even mention them.

The Carnival/Lent opposition between the narrator and Severin Winter is not so clear-cut. Although Severin is a sobering influence on the couples—his name, like others in Irving's fiction, is playfully allusive—he is by no means a personality of Lenten virtue. He agrees to the exchange of sexual partners because he feels that he owes it to Edith; he had an affair some years earlier, and his agreement is his way of making things even. But Severin is difficult. Even at the beginning of the relationship the narrator writes, "it was Severin who could never give the four of us a chance. . . . He was uncomfortable, so he tried to make us uncomfortable too." In a central episode, when the couples decide to spend an orgiastic weekend on Cape Cod, Severin sees it as "just a holiday," and cautions, "We should be careful no one gets too excited." He sums up his feelings when he speaks of the futility of having "a little nothing relationship": "I mean, if you have one good relationship, why would you be interested in having a little nothing of a relationship?" Later he adds,

> "I honestly admit the degree of independence that I *don't* have if I live with someone . . . and I expect whoever's living with me to do the same." (Later I remember him yelling: "There's a precious amount of having-one's-cake-and-eating-it-too shit going on around here.")

Whereas Severin does present a troubled, responsible reaction (strengthened somewhat by the narrator's presentation of it) to the sexual exchange, he is not a wholly admirable character. He is nearly related to Bruegel's presentation of Lent, which implies that false piety is no better than dissolute living —beyond the narrator's biased account, Irving's novel thus preserves the balance of Bruegel's painting. The inescapable facts are that Severin has had an affair and that he does agree to the *ménage à quatre*. Also, he hurts Utch by merely going through the motions with her while she falls in love with him. As this duplicity demonstrates, Severin, too, is an egocentric and selfish man. His acquiescence in the mate swapping, further, stems primarily from his discomfort at Edith's being one-up on him on the register of infidelity. Real equality in a sexual relationship upsets him: prior to the exchange, he mentions to Edith one morning that he is thinking of having an affair, and when she admits to having the same thoughts, he becomes angry. He is extremely vain, according to the narrator, "too vain to be jealous," and this is true. His unemotional, almost clinical, involvement in the *ménage* becomes disturbing and tends to balance the sympathy-producing aspects of his announced scruples.

Part of Severin's problem is his inability to free himself of his mother. At one point the narrator comments, "I think Severin thought about his mother too much"—his bedroom in Vienna and later his bedroom in America (after his marriage) is decorated with paintings of his mother in various erotic positions, masturbating. Intimately connected with this is Severin's love for the wrestling room, his own private world. It is described as a womblike enclosure, safe from the reality of the world. It is in the wrestling room that he meets and courts Audrey Canon—it is this affair which precipitates the *ménage*. Audrey Canon is a former dancer who lost part of her foot in an accident; Severin thinks that she is beautiful and claims her "beauty was in her grace, which was in her past. He claimed that he could love a person's past." His preoccupation with the past, and with Audrey Canon's "grace" links her in a way with his mother, an Oedipal connection that Severin cannot seem to overcome. Severin's affair with Audrey Canon ends when Edith finds them in the wrestling room—later she will discover that he has taken Utch there as well. Significantly, both of Severin's wrestling-room lovers are linked to the past—Utch to Austria, Audrey to his mother.

The wrestling room (like Cyril's Illyria) exists for Severin as a kind of imaginative construct, a place where he can be his ideal self, a place where reality does not intrude. Here he can live a strange and, to him, sensual dream, divorced from the world that he finds alien and hostile. In this light a comment he makes about his children is important:

He said they were his substitute for an adventurous, explorative life. With children his life would always be dangerous. . . . He said his love for Edith was almost rational (a matter of definition, I suppose), but that there was nothing reasonable about the way he loved his children. He said that people who didn't have children were naïve about the control they had over their lives.

This is a typical Irving protagonist's attitude toward children, but it also reveals something relevant to Severin's other involvement: for him the *ménage* is dangerous because he cannot control it. There are too many separate lives involved. That is why his wrestling-room seems safe for him; it is a one-on-one situation, like the sport of wrestling itself. But in the four-way affair, Severin does not know how to exercise control. The narrator writes: "I have seen how his wrestlers look at their opponents with a cold, analytical scrutiny, a dead eye. Severin Winter gave me such a look. Though he couldn't have been oblivious to the ridiculousness of his controlled behavior, he cherished the idea!" It is this very idealistic quality about Severin that makes him difficult to deal with, and makes the continuation of the affair impossible.

Only when Severin goes back to the wrestling room—like Plato's cave—can he revert to a baser state. He himself understands this analogy, for his wrestlers enact Plato's parable of emerging from darkness to light before each match:

> He looked them all up and down, as if he could see in the darkness. *"Wie gehts?"* he'd ask them; in the tunnel, his voice boomed. . . . They were all his German students, you see.
>
> And in unison the wrestlers would bellow in that tunnel, *"Gut!"*
>
> Then Winter would fling open the door, and like moles emerging into daylight, his wrestlers would blindly follow him into the new gym and startling light and yelling crowd and out onto that shining crimson and white wrestling mat. To the spectators they always

looked as if they had been brainwashed in a dungeon and sent out on some grim task into the real world. They *had*.

It is Winter's desire to return to the wrestling room— the cave is for Plato a place that keeps out the light of the sun—that counterbalances his idealism. In the dark room a wrestler can regress to a purely physical state, where, as Severin says, "If you think, you realize you can lose—and you're right."

In this light, three events that befall Severin near the end of the novel are particularly significant. Each year he takes his best wrestlers to a championship meet at Oklahoma State University. This year his star, George James Bender, wins all of his preliminary matches and then becomes inexplicably listless and loses his final match. It is eventually revealed that Edith tried to seduce Bender and that "he just didn't get up for it." He was so humiliated that he was unable to wrestle well the next day—Bender's experience with the light of the real world has destroyed his cave mentality. After this episode, Severin resigns as wrestling coach.

During a dinner party with the narrator and Utch sometime later, the Winters' children are badly cut when the glass door of a bathtub falls in on them. This is the central violent episode of the novel:

> The bathroom looked like the scene of a gang-land slaying. The old door had pitched into the tub and broken over the naked girls, the glass exploding from the frame, sending shards and fragments flying every-where; it crunched under Severin's shoes as he plunged his arms into the tub. The tub was pink, the water bloody; you could not tell who was cut where.

In resigning as wrestling coach, Severin has given up the world of the cave and restated his claim to the world outside. However, in Irving's universe the light of the outside is not the ideal described by Plato in *The Republic,* but a world in which there is no control, where "danger is everywhere." The children's accident enforces this fact upon Severin, while also serving, as such violence regularly does in Irving's fiction, as a punishment for his (and Edith's) faithlessness.

Severin's final act is taking Edith to the wrestling room, in which symbolic act his darker self is sublimated and he renews his connection with the more responsible part of his nature. He seems ready now for a life of commitment to his wife and to his family. The healing process having begun, Severin then joins his family in Vienna, a place where he once learned the lessons of danger, but also a place where truces "run long and deep."

The character who suffers most from the whole experience is Utch. Like Severin, she is a child of pain and suffering, but the affair further scars her, and at the end she leaves her husband and goes to Vienna with her two sons. The narrator has remarked that his wife "could teach patience to a time-bomb," her childhood experience having taught her that. When she came to America with her husband on the day of President Kennedy's assassination, she alone remained unaffected: "In Europe of course, they kill their aristocracy all the time, but not in America. . . . For Utch, I suppose, it was not at all unusual; it was the way they would settle scores in Eichbüchl. Nobody had taught her to expect any other part of the world to behave differently." Unlike the Americans in Irving's world, who are continually surprised and shocked, Utch has learned the lessons of history first-hand, and she is better able to apply this long-range perspective to her own life than her husband, who only speculates about history and its meanings.

Unfortunately, despite the fact that her past is well detailed, Utch does not emerge as a convincing character during the course of the novel. Things seem to happen to her—she mostly gets drunk and falls asleep—though she does rouse herself to fall in love with Severin Winter. Their relationship is largely a matter of speculation, owing to its development beyond the range of the first-person narrator, but it seems likely that their similar backgrounds must have led to a degree of natural understanding and sympathy of feeling greater than she has ever found in her husband. By the end of the novel she has come to understand her husband as well, however, and when the affair is over she dismisses their marriage bitterly with the remark that "You know *you* . . . that's all you know." Thus Utch, who was made so vivid a figure in the account of her childhood experience, presents once again, as she decides to leave her husband, a strong and definable impression, but the effect is not consistent throughout the novel, as her thoughts and responses in the midst of the affair remain too sketchy to convey her development in character. It is a serious flaw in a book whose central focus—and considerable achievement, in the cases of the other three principals —is dynamic characterization.

The narrator, as mentioned earlier, learns nothing; unlike any of Irving's other protagonists, he remains too preoccupied with himself to gain any useful perspective on the experience he has been reviewing in his narrative. He never achieves the "wide-angle view." Despite the fact that he provides the perceptive reader enough information from which to draw some conclusions, the narrator himself cannot seem to piece this information together meaningfully. His summary description of Bruegel's painting and his presentation of his own story demonstrate that he can gather facts and that he has a perceptive eye for detail, but his understanding is so limited that he remains ignorant of the larger patterns of his own life. By the end of the novel, his family has left him and his father has died, but he feels nothing. He concludes the novel with characteristic insouciance:

> Yesterday Utch wrote that she saw Edith sitting in Demel's eating a pastry. I hope she gets fat.
> So. Today I bought a plane ticket. My mother gave me the money. If cuckolds catch a second wind, I am eagerly waiting for mine.

Presumably he will learn little in Vienna, either.

*The 158-Pound Marriage* is a very consciously styled novel, rich in literary and artistic allusions, and narrated by a writer who occasionally comments on the art of writing itself. In one of his discussions of fiction with Edith, he mentions a colleague who is also a novelist:

> . . . Helmbart's sort of haughty kingship over what was called "the new novel" was nauseating to me. Edith and I agreed that when the subject of fiction became how to write fiction, we lost interest; we were interested in prose, surely, but not when the subject of the prose became prose itself.

He speaks here for Irving, who is a strong advocate of the traditional novel. However, the narrator/Irving is hedging here just a little, for although this novel is a traditional novel—concerned with real time, character development, and plot—it is also very modern in its concern for the fictional process itself. Much of its complexity derives from the manipulation of its narrative by two separate novelists: the narrator and Irving himself, and whereas this dual structuring provides some of its most interesting effects, it is also the novel's central weakness. Irving simply fails to

employ the first person consistently; too often the
narrator seems to be speaking directly for Irving,
from outside his own personality—this was also noticeable in Siggy's journal in Part Two of *Setting Free
the Bears,* wherein the reflections on history clearly
emerged from a different mind than that reflected in
the Siggy of the earlier section. Irving does not seem
to possess, in these early novels, the discipline to
sustain a first-person narrative by leaving the telling
to his character. When this narrator is discussing
Austrian or Russian history, he, too generally lapses
into Irving's voice:

> On July 9, 1945, the Allies quartered the city of Vienna
> for occupation. The Americans and British grabbed up
> the best residential sections, the French took over the
> markets and the major shopping areas, and the Rus-
> sians (who had long-term, realistic plans) settled in the
> worker-industrial districts and within the Inner City,
> nearest to the embassies and the government buildings.
> During the carving of the great game bird, the dinner
> guests revealed their special tastes.

Again, when he recounts Kudashvili's leaving Utch to
fight in Hungary:

> It was the good people of Budapest who freed her.
> On October 25, 1956, a lot of people's good intentions
> were upset. The Hungarians did not feel that because
> Russia had liberated them from the Nazis they owed
> the Russians anything as unreasonably large as their
> country.

This tone is very close to that in many of the passages
in Siggy's journal; it is even more out of place here
because Irving has made it clear that the narrator
does not have the perception to write this way about
history. This inability to sustain his narrator's voice,

which consititutes this novel's major flaw, will at last
be corrected in *Garp*, another novel about a novelist,
in which Irving will revert to the third person and set
off Garp's writing in special sections which interrupt
the main narrative. Here, however, Irving comes
closer to Helmbart than he may realize, flirting playfully with reflexivity, while yet maintaining his essential allegiance to traditional form.

Another of the novel's weaknesses is the constant
reliance upon wrestling metaphors, as the narrator
adopts them from Severin's speech. Occasionally
amusing, they recur too frequently to function as an
effective, or even illuminating, literary device. The
title of the novel derives from this tendency, and it is
(rather obscurely) significant in terms of the novel's
central theme. In college, it seems, Severin wrestled
in the 157-pound class (later raised to 158 pounds),
which is the middleweight category. Wrestlers, however, do not compete at their natural body weights,
but at lower weights maintained by constant dieting
and exercise; the loss of pounds does not affect
muscle strength, which thus becomes a great advantage in the lower weight classes.[8] In other words, the
wrestler exists in a constant limbo world, striving to
combine a weight that is not natural with a muscle
strength that is, and fighting in a weight class which
thus does not reflect a measurable reality.

The characters in the novel occupy just such a
limbo world, as they try to achieve an unnatural
relationship, while attempting to sustain a natural
one. But the limbo world of Irving's universe is more
profound and frightening than that: at one point the
narrator, in one of his many literary allusions, refers
to Djuna Barnes's *Nightwood*, another novel about a
multifaceted relationship, in which one of the characters remarks, "Man was born damned and innocent
from the start, and wretchedly—as he must—on these

themes—whistles his tune."[8] Irving's characters must also deal with this difficult dualism, maintaining their "weight class" in a modern world bereft of meaning and affording them no support. Writing on Barnes, Louis Kannenstine makes a point that applies equally well to Irving: "The characters, as they move between the dualities of existence, must either suffer without comprehending or collapse under an intolerable burden of understanding. The essence of the whole work, then, is enigma."[9] Ultimately Irving, and not his narrator, suggests that the essence of his work is enigma as well—in the painting which mirrors the novel's thematic concerns, Bruegel centers a couple being led down a path by a fool, equidistant between Carnival and Lent. Irving's narrator may, in fact, be such a fool, and many of his characters do suffer without comprehending, but his more preceptive ones do not collapse. Some, like Severin Winter, learn to recognize the enigma and to grapple doggedly with its moral challenge.

# CHAPTER 5

## Portrait of the Artist as a Nervous Wreck

When T. S. Garp gives one of his early stories to his girl friend Helen, he is at first hurt—and then made even more determined to become a great writer—by her critique: "This story shows promise, although I do think, at this point, you are more of a wrestler than a writer." Whereas Irving's own first three novels demonstrate too much developing talent to be dismissed simply as "wrestling," they are, nevertheless, a working out, a movement toward a design and an imaginative rendering of a world view. *The World According to Garp*, on the other hand, seems a kind of culmination, the completion of a phase in Irving's career. This, his fourth novel, serves in one respect as a summary glance backward at that career, for its protagonist Garp, himself a writer, pursues a course that closely parallels that of his creator, even to the writing of two novels that resemble *Setting Free the Bears* and *The 158-Pound Marriage*. Irving does not resort to such repetition of materials in order to build some mythical world like Faulkner's, but out of an apparent need to come to grips with them himself. He seems to have to revisit the places, review the history, and re-create the people from various different angles, along the way adding, discarding, and refining, in a progressive struggle toward some balanced, comprehensive hold on the themes and energies that pervade his fiction. In *Garp*, Irving manages to shape his familiar material into a transcendent whole, and in doing so fashions his best and most original work. *The World According to Garp* is thus at once a personal masterpiece, an important contemporary artifact, a clear explication of Irving's moral and aesthetic vision, and a certification of his talent. It signals the arrival of a writer in full command of his abilities, entering upon the mature phase of his career.

This novel reintroduces places, motifs, and themes familiar to readers of Irving's first three novels: Vienna, a small New England college town, wrestling, bears, marital infidelity, the protection of children, violence, and death. In *Garp*, however, these customary elements are newly combined and their association made suddenly significant. Here Irving has harnessed both dimensions of his talent, merging the astute observer of a world ruled by mishap and chance and the chaotic record of its history with the writer of compassion and tenderness —previously most evident in *The Water-Method Man*— who refuses to give in to our "age of enormity."

*Garp*, a novel whose plot resists brief summary, is rich in compassion, although it is, at the same time, Irving's most consistently violent tale. A story full of murder and mutilation, its thematic focus is on making things whole. It is a book about people who cut out their tongues and can't speak, and yet more than any of his other novels, it concerns the act of articulation and mankind's desperate need to communicate wisely. T. S. Garp emerges gradually as a true hero in an age without heroes, for his life is an obesssive attempt to make a threatening world safe for his family and a widening circle of friends and dependents; his occasionally misdirected methods are foresight and precaution, communication, and understanding through imagination and tolerance.

Like Siggy and Trumper, Garp is a writer, and like the unnamed narrator of *The 158-Pound Marriage*, a novelist as well. Unlike the narrator, however, Garp's concern is the imagination, not history. Indeed, one problem he must contend with during the novel is an inability to separate his own personal life from his fiction and so achieve what Wordsworth called "the visionary gleam." When, at last, he does ver come his imaginative block, he feels liberated and triumphant. Whereas that earlier narrator, only a marginally imaginative man, molded his plots on a narrow fidelity to historical fact, producing a type of novel alien to Garp's sensibility, Garp is a thoroughly eccentric creator who concentrates exclusively on his art—he has no other job, not even a teaching position like that of the narrator of the *The 158-Pound Marriage*.

*The World According to Garp* is Irving's most traditional novel, recounting the life story of a man, his family, his friends, and his world. All this is presented in a fairly straightforward, chronological manner, detailing Garp's unorthodox origin, his schooling, his experience in Vienna, his marriage, his family life, his literary career, and his death. Along the way Irving also provides complete histories of Garp's mother, Jenny Fields, his wife Helen, and his best friend, Roberta Muldoon, as well as convincing portraits of his three children and his editor, John Wolf. Most important, in this his most ambitious novel, Irving takes on the world. Speaking to Duncan Garp about his father's career, Wolf remarks, "He started out daring to write about the *world*—when he was just a *kid*, for Christ's sake, he still took it on." This, too, is Irving's task in *Garp*, not only to take on the world and understand it but also to re-create it, representing its promises and its dangers, in accordance with his own vision.

Comprehension of the world is the main subject of this novel, and the coming to an understanding is Garp's personal quest. In many ways, *Garp* is a *Bildungsroman*, the story of a boy's maturing into a man by learning to deal with the world around him. The title itself announces the need to shape the world into a vision, and in the novel Garp considers and adapts various visions—the world according to Marcus Aurelius, to Bensenhaver, to Grillparzer—building on them to create a vision of his own. Throughout much of the novel, however, this comprehension remains elusive, as Garp is a man surrounded by chaos and violence, which frustrate his search for some pattern of meaning and frequently force his fictions into dead ends and stagnation.

Late in the novel Duncan Garp reminisces with his father about past summers spent in the family house on the New Hampshire coast. Garp then would often warn Walt, his younger son, about the undertow of the current along the shore, reminding him that "the undertow is strong today," or "the undertow is wicked today." When Walt was four years old, Garp and Helen noticed him apparently studying the sea; asked what he was doing, Walt replied, "I'm trying to see the Under Toad"—having mistaken his parents' term, the child thus in his imagination mythicized the force into some "terrible" being waiting to "suck him under and drag him out to sea." In Garp's life, thereafter, the Under Toad becomes a "code phrase for anxiety," but it actually functions much more powerfully throughout the novel—it is the incarnation of mishap and the irrational, concretizing and symbolizing the forces that disrupt human life and sometimes destroy it *(tod* is the German word for death). Indeed, the Under Toad is everywhere in Irving's world: it controls history in *Setting Free the Bears,* and it troubles the lives of all of Irving's protagonists. It becomes Garp's aim—as it is Irving's —to come to grips with the Under Toad and so learn to deal with it, and in the words of one critic, "to fix the perception of life's demonic undertow at exactly those points where, any day, any one of us might slip and be sucked down."[1]

Intimately connected with the concept of the Under Toad and the need to grapple with it is the influence on the novel of Marcus Aurelius's *Meditations.* Aurelius, emperor of Rome (A.D. 161–180), who wrote his *Meditations* during his campaigns against the barbarians, was a Stoic philosopher, although his work is not pure Stoic philosophy. The Stoics believed in the necessity of striving after wisdom, which they defined as knowledge of the divine and human; the aim of the philosopher was to live in harmony with nature. If one could gain knowledge or wisdom and live in harmony with nature, then one was virtuous. Such virtue was the only good, and not being virtuous in this way was the only evil.

Although much of the *Meditations* consists of instructions in the right way to live, what distinguishes them is Aurelius's struggle to reconcile himself with death and with the recurrent notion that the universe might, indeed, rest on ungoverned chaos— that rather than divine providence, ultimate meaning might depend upon some inexorable destiny that is impossible to resist. The philosopher's dilemma, then, was how to maintain his belief in divine provi dence and order in face of the destruction he could not but witness around him, how to accommodate the horrors into some kind of scheme.

Aurelius' observation at the end of Book II has a profound effect on Garp:

> In the life of a man, his time is but a moment, his being an incessant flux, his senses a dim rushlight, his body a prey of worms, his soul an unquiet eddy, his fortune dark, and his fame doubtful. In short, all that is of the body is as coursing waters, all that is of the soul as dreams and vapors; life a warfare, a brief sojourning in an alien land; and after repute, oblivion.[2]

Garp reads the *Meditations* in Vienna, the place of Aurelius's death, and even as a teenager he understands that "the subject of Marcus Aurelius's dreary observations was certainly the subject of most serious writing." This dark philosophy, and especially Aurelius's obsession with death, deeply influences young Garp, whose first story is about death—also a central concern of Irving's novel. In addition, Aurelius's cyclical theory of history, suggesting that everything repeats itself in endless cosmic cycles, clarifies not only Garp's developing world view but also Irving's conviction that history must be studied and understood if its warnings and its signals are not to be lost.

In a very Irving-like metaphor, Aurelius counsels against the Under Toad: "The art of living is more like wrestling than dancing, in as much as it, too, demands a firm and watchful stance against any unexpected onset."[3] (Like Garp, a father, Aurelius lost four children—Garp loses one—and he warned "While you are kissing your child, Epictetus once said, murmur under your breath, tomorrow it may be dead."[4]) Irving's novel encompasses the duality of Aurelius's problem, the need to structure a world and to maintain vigilance in a world that seems to defy comprehension, the overwhelming need to create or maintain unity out of seeming disunity. In the final book of the *Meditations,* Aurelius masters his fears and reconciles the apparent divisions he sees; Garp, too, will at last learn to structure his world, and in facing the worst, like Aurelius, will also become reconciled.

It almost seems that the method of Garp's conception in part determines his world view. His mother, Jenny Fields, an heiress born into society, decides to live her own life and turns her back on her family. Being in tune with one's own nature (a prominent concept in the *Meditations)* and living according to it in one's own world is a major theme in *Garp,* and Jenny Fields, fiercely independent, does indeed create her own world. As a child she studied clams—"It was the first live thing she understood completely—its life, its sex, its death."—and when she becomes a nurse, she discovers "that people weren't much more mysterious, or more attractive than clams." Working in a Boston hospital, she also learns a great deal about injury, death, and birth. Having dealt with pregnant women who did not want their babies and with diseases, she develops a strong distaste for sex and decides to live a life without sex, although she wants a child. In her autobiography, *A Sexual Suspect,* she later summarizes her desires and her independence: "I wanted a job and I wanted to live alone. That made me a sexual suspect. Then I wanted a baby, but I didn't want to have to share my body or my life to have one. That made me a sexual suspect, too." Her colleagues tease her about her wish for a kind of virgin birth: "Old Virgin Mary Jenny . . . doesn't want a baby the easy way. Why not ask God for one?" Jenny does, indeed, manage an almost virgin birth, and Irving makes no effort to disguise the Virgin Mary parallels—both woman are "sexual suspects," celibate, and heroically generous; both lose their sons at the age of thirty-three.

Jenny works in a ward that sees only "terminal cases," and so the influence of death, especially violent death, is to be felt very early in the novel. She labels her patients as "externals" (victims of burns), "vital organs" (those shot and damaged internally), "absentees" ("men who weren't 'there' anymore"), and "goners." Garp's father, a ball turret gunner who has been badly wounded in the war and a man "whose familiarity with violent death cannot be exaggerated," is classified not only a "goner" but also an "external" (his hands are burned), a "vital organ" (he has sustained brain damage and other internal destruction), and an "absentee." Technical Sergeant Garp, in other words, is no more than some wrapped-up flesh, barely alive and able only to articulate the word "Garp." Then even this last faculty deteriorates —as his condition worsens, his one-word vocabulary diminishes progressively to "Arp," then "Ar," then "A." When he has only one vowel and one consonant left, Jenny in a sense rapes him, giving Garp a last moment of pleasure. Afterwards he regresses to a womblike state: ". . . he resumed a fetal position, tucked up small in the center of the bed. He made no sound at all." Soon afterwards, he dies.

The elder Garp's death and his final regression are meant to recall Randall Jarrell's "The Death of the Ball Turret Gunner," which is short enough to be reproduced here in its entirety:

> From my mother's sleep I fell into the State,
> And I hunched in its belly till my wet fur froze.
> Six miles from earth, loosed from its dream of life,
> I woke to black flak and the nightmare fighters.

When I died they washed me out of the turret with a
hose.[5]

Jarrell's image of the dreamer waking to a horrible
reality is reversed in *Garp*. Irving maintains the
turret/womb parallel, but Technical Sergeant Garp
goes from his turret back to the womb, giving life to
his son with one "last shot" before he dies. In permit-
ting this last affirmative and creative act, Irving
significantly emends Jarrell, whose poem implies that
there is nothing between birth and violent death.

Irving's elaborate detailing of his protagonist's
birth echoes also Laurence Sterne's *The Life and
Opinions of Tristram Shandy*, which also chronicles its
hero's life from the moment of conception. Tristram,
who narrates the novel, is as deeply affected by the
circumstances of his genesis as is Garp, and even
more conscious of their indelible influence upon his
character:

I wish either my father or my mother, or indeed both
of them . . . had minded what they were about when
they begot me. . . . Had they duly weighed and considered all this, and proceeded accordingly—I am verily
persuaded I should have made a quite different figure
in the world, from that in which the reader is likely to
see me.[6]

Irving's debt to his eighteenth-century predecessor is
more important, however, than mere plot similarity,
for in thus echoing *Tristram Shandy*—T. S., in fact, is
the initial/name that is his own hero's inheritance
from his father—he is also promising that his tale is to
be more than some nihilistic exercise in dramatizing
violence and death. Both novels, to be sure, are full of
violent incident and fatality—the concentration on
physical maiming is particularly noticeable—and yet

both writers place primary emphasis on the constructive feelings of their characters and the spirit of affirmation inherent in their behavior. In *Tristram Shandy*, this ennobling focus is achieved principally through the character of My Uncle Toby; in *Garp*, it is achieved primarily through Jenny Fields and Garp himself. Most importantly, both writers dedicate their art—employing common tactics of game playing, broad comedy, narrative manipulation, and deliberate digression—to overcoming the chaos and the horror that their stories reflect. Both Sterne and Irving declare their freedom from the specter of death by laughing at it and playing with it, both dealing with bizarre events and insisting that laughter is "a species of sympathy."[7] (Irving's original title for his novel—it is used in the novel as the title of Garp's biography—was *Lunacy and Sorrow,* a recognition of this basic ambivalence.)

Even as a child Garp begins to exhibit the temperament and mind set that will characterize his adult vision. Raised in a rather closed environment, a New England boys' prep school where his mother works as a nurse, he early comes in contact with injury and disease and develops an interest in them: "Garp liked the athletic injuries best; he liked looking at casts and slings and big bandages, and he liked listening to the cause of the injury, over and over again." An early childhood mishap demonstrates to Garp the precarious nature of life: chasing pigeons on the infirmary roof one evening, he falls through a rain gutter, severely cuts his leg, and then hangs from the edge of the roof. Later, in the hospital, he thinks for the first time about the Under Toad: "Garp felt a darkness surround him, akin to the darkness and sense of being far away that he must have felt while lying in the rain gutter, four stories above where the world was safe." Shortly after this episode, Garp is more

seriously maimed when a neighbor's oddly hostile
dog bites off part of his ear.

As a student at the Steering School, Garp displays the "powerful discipline" necessary for a writer,
as well as an innate single-mindedness of purpose:
"From the beginning he appeared to believe there
was something strenuous to achieve." His attitude
and instinct for a personal aesthetic is expressed at
age fifteen in an essay on athletics: "I do not care for
balls. The ball stands between the athlete and his
exercise. . . . And when one further removes one's
body from the contest by an extension device—such
as a racquet, a bat, or a stick—all purity of movement,
strength, and focus is lost."

Because of this, Garp, like Severin Winter, joins
the wrestling team: "He loved the singleness of the
combat, and the frightening confines of that circle
inscribed on the mat; the terrific conditioning; the
mental constancy of keeping his weight down." The
wrestling room also functions for Garp, as it did in
*The 158-Pound Marriage,* as a haven, a place of safety.
Jenny, on her visit to the Steering wrestling room,
feels the peculiar lure of the place; asking herself,
"why do I feel so *safe* here?", she recognizes it as an
environment that is "padded against pain," a substitute womb where her child may seemingly be protected from the more pointed hazards of the world
without. Even after his Steering days, Garp will
return to wrestling rooms; ironically, he will also die
in one.

It is in the wrestling room that Garp meets the
coach's daughter, Helen Holm, and falls in love:
"There in the warm red wrestling room, on the soft
mats, surrounded by those padded walls—in such an
environment, sudden and inexplicable closeness is
possible." A voracious reader and a student of literature, Helen tells Garp that if she marries anybody it

will be a "real writer." Promptly he decides to become one, and with the stubborn devotion that he brings to all his interests, sets out to become a "real writer."

In the two chapters devoted to Garp's Steering days, Irving concentrates on the four concerns that preoccupy both Garp and the novel: writing, wrestling, sex, and death. Regularly throughout the novel, Irving will present a character and then provide a quick glimpse into the future to prefigure that person's death—Garp's mentor and English teacher, Tinch, for example, is introduced with the assurance that he is destined to die by freezing to death some years later. The Under Toad is everywhere in the novel, and Irving thus forces his reader to confront it constantly.

In the chapter entitled "Graduation" Irving also links sex and death, a dominant motif in the novel. Garp's first brush with sex, an encounter with Cushing Percy, is not an entirely successful one, as she demurs at his failure to produce contraceptives— Garp's first sexual experience therefore becomes, significantly, an oral one. While they are together, however, Garp and Cushy observe her father and a friend on the other side of the river playing golf. When the friend steps into the muddy water and is trapped, Irving presents the incident as another powerful evocation of the Under Toad: "He moved forward on the trunk of his body, using his arms the way a seal on land will use its flippers. An awful *slorp*ing noise pursued him through the mud flats, as if beneath the mud some mouth was gasping to suck him in."

When Garp finally does manage sex with Cushy, on his graduation night, there are ironic echoes of his parents' relationship, for it is done in the infirmary near the rooms for surgery and anesthesia—"The odor would stay in his mind as deeply personal and yet and vaguely *hospital.*" Sex for Garp thereafter becomes "a solitary act committed in an abandoned universe," but also "an act of terrific optimism." Although his first sexual experience is an affirmative one, it will lead, eventually, to his death at the hands of Cushy's crazed sister. Sex is thus both a redemptive and a death-bringing force, as will be most forcefully demonstrated later in the novel, when Helen and Garp have their most violent encounter with the Under Toad, the loss of their son Walt.

On the advice of Tinch, Garp and Jenny go to Vienna after his graduation. Garp is to learn there about the world and to prepare himself for being a writer. Here Irving produces his fullest explication of the complex impression made upon him by the city that has figured so prominently in all of his novels. For Garp, Vienna is an ideal city to study, profoundly affecting his imagination and helping him form his "scheme of things," something he understands a writer must have. Writing to Helen, he likens it to "a museum housing a dead city"—indeed it seems a city frozen in time, a place that can be examined and from which his vision can be gleaned: "A more real city might not have suited me so well . . . but Vienna was in its death phase; it lay still and let me look at it, and think about it, and look again. In a *living* city, I could never have noticed so much. Living cities don't hold still." It is at this time that Garp reads Marcus Aurelius, whose credo, "all that is body is as coursing waters," deeply affects him and which he repeats to himself often—it summarizes for Garp the essence of Vienna, sparking his imagination and laying the groundwork for his first "real" story.

Garp also reads the work of a famous Viennese, Franz Grillparzer (1791–1872,) who becomes his model for what a writer should not be. Grillparzer's most famous prose work, *The Poor Fiddler,* is considered one of the great works of the Austrian imagination—Ivar Ivask has written that "Austrian literature has been attracted time and time again to a kind of baroque realism, characterized by a constant tension between illusion and reality, being and doing. It is an essential tension that is to be borne, if not in faith, then at least with stoical equanimity. . . ."[8] This tension pervades *The Poor Fiddler,* and, the *Meditations* as well. Aurelius wrote the lines that meant so much to Garp in Vienna; baroque realism is also a style that, in part, characterizes *The World According to Garp.*

Grillparzer's hero, Jacob, is a forerunner of the modern superfluous man: a failure in practical life, unable to deal with hostile reality, though pure in spirit and a confirmed idealist. For Garp, Grillparzer is unable to bring off his story despite the seriousness of the subject matter because his treatment seems ludicrously melodramatic and "baldly sentimental"—he remarks that "Dostoevsky . . . could compel you to be interested in such a wretch; Grillparzer bored you with tearful trivia." Irving's novel, too, often verges on sentimentality and melodrama, but he carefully tempers that tendency with comic inventiveness, and so his work does avoid the triteness of *The Poor Fiddler.* Later in the novel, in writing to an outraged reader, Garp defends his own work and his method of dealing with life's paradoxes, and his argument seems to summarize Irving's art as well:

> . . . I have never understood why 'serious' and 'funny' are thought to be opposites. It is simply a truthful contradiction to me that people's problems are often funny and that the people are often and nonetheless sad.
>
> . . . I take people very seriously. People are all I

take seriously, in fact. Therefore, I have nothing but
sympathy for how people behave—and nothing but
laughter to console them with.

In his first story Garp successfully balances comedy
and compassion—as Irving's narrator comments,
"The story did not belittle the *people* in the story
—either with forced cuteness or with any other
exaggeration rationalized as necessary for making a
point. Neither did the story sentimentalize the people, or otherwise cheapen their sadness." One of
Garp's problems later will be his inability to sustain
this imaginative balance and so preserve the creative
tension in his art.

As a very young man Garp is confident and in
full control. Aurelius, Grillparzer, and Vienna stimulate and shape his imagination; another important
influence is a whore named Charlotte with whom
Garp has sex and also develops a close friendship. In
this relationship sex and death are linked again, as,
despite Charlotte's carefully preserved exterior
appearance—". . . only when she was completely un-
dressed was her age apparent anywhere except in the
veins on her long hands"—her internal organs are
being gradually ravaged by disease. In a sense, then,
the proud but aging whore stands as the very embodiment of the city of Vienna, which is the young Garp's
spiritual mistress—clinging to the memory of a glam-
orous past, while hiding the scars occasioned by its
less glorious moments, she ends up at last in a hospital
ward for terminal cases. When Garp visits her there,
she has lost her sex organs, her breasts, and much of
her digestive tract; she dies shortly thereafter. Garp
realizes then that "the subject of the great painters in
the great museums was always death," and Vienna
seems even more "ripe with dying" than usual. But
consistent with the duality of experience that per-

vades the novel, this death, too, leads to birth—in Garp's case imaginative birth, expressed in the completion of his first story, "The Pension Grillparzer."

This story reflects young Garp's vision of the world—heavily influenced by his Viennese experience—imaginatively re-created: "Garp was savoring . . . the beginning of a writer's long-sought trance, wherein the world falls under one embracing tone of voice." The title refers ironically to Franz Grillparzer, whose name is here given to a Grade C pension; it points as well to a likeness in style and theme. The story is baroque, its situations and incidents exaggerated and wildly imaginative; the tension between illusion and reality (Grillparzer's characteristic theme) is skillfully maintained. A fantastical portrait of the city that fascinates him—"the Pension Grillparzer" can only be Vienna itself—this work teems with symbolic references to the exotic appeal and the ill-concealed decadence of that city. Briefly, the tale is narrated by a young man who travels around Austria with his family, helping his father rate restaurants, hotels, and pensions. The Pension Grillparzer has a C rating and aspires to a B, but it is found to be inhabited by a bizarre menagerie—a man who walks on his hands, a bear who rides a unicycle, and a man who recounts other people's dreams—and so the effort for reclassification is hopeless. The whole episode is finally summed up by the narrator as "a ludicrous and doomed effort at reclassification."

At the heart of the story lurk death and the Under Toad. The narrator's grandmother has a recurrent dream, which is recounted by the interpreter as a dream of death; it deals with Charlemagne's soldiers drinking from a frozen fountain, horses with "long masks of ice on their muzzles," and men gnawing at their dead companions' bones. Years before, when the grandmother first had this dream, her husband died, and after this experience at the pension, the grandmother also dies. The story, through a kind of epilogue, also recounts the deaths of the narrator's parents, his brother Robo, the owner of the pension, and the man who walks on his hands, who, in a particularly vivid image of the Under Toad, has been strangled to death when his necktie became caught in an escalator.

The central symbol in the story is the bear, Duna (the Hungarian name for the Danube), who lives in the human environment of the pension, rides a unicycle, and even uses the W.C. Later, however, Duna's habits grow indecent, and it is consigned to a cage, where it is taunted by children and dogs, and, finally, to the Schönbrunn zoo, where it develops rheumatism and a rash and eventually dies. "His long history of having been treated as a human being did not prepare him for the gentler routine of zoo life." The bear, like the pension, cannot be reclassified. Unable at last to live in the human world, Duna cannot exist even as a bear. Like Grillparzer's fiddler, the bear can neither live in the world nor transcend its own state, and so it dies a miserable death.

Duna is also like Austria: toothless, clawless, victimized by the Russians, and unable to adjust to its limbolike existence. A nation at the crossroads of other nations, Austria had found itself unable to organize against the threatening influence of Nazi Germany, and so was taken over by Hitler and later plundered by the Allies, especially Russia. For Garp, present-day Austria, in consequence, is a place without a present:

> Not many Viennese were born in 1943; for that matter, not many Viennese were born from the start of the Nazi occupation in 1938 through the end of the war in 1945. And although there were a surprising number of

babies born out of rapes, not many Viennese *wanted*
babies until after 1955—the end of the Russian occupation. Vienna was a city occupied by foreigners for
seventeen years. . . . It was Garp's experience to live in
a city that made him feel peculiar to be eighteen years
old.

Vienna is a place caught between a conception of the
ideal—it was once the center of the Holy Roman
Empire—and its reality. Like Charlotte, the whore,
vowing proudly to retire "at the first sign that her
first-district appeal was slipping," the capital city
vainly strives to resist reclassification by hiding its
inner decay behind a facade of artificial polish, but it,
too, is moribund, its insides grotesquely wasted and
degenerate. Garp's vision, like Grillparzer's, is a dark
one; no transcendence, reclassification, or triumph
seems possible, and man is shown as a puppet whose
destiny depends upon a whimsical fate. As Helen
later remarks of the story, in its conclusion "we can
glimpse what the world according to Garp would be
like."

While Garp is spending his time learning about
the city and writing, Jenny prepares her own autobiography, which will make her a wealthy celebrity.
After more than a year in Vienna, they return to
America, and Garp marries Helen. He then begins
his literary career in earnest, at the same time cooking
and looking after their two sons while Helen works as
a university professor.

Despite Irving's protests against the reflexivity of
the modern novel, in *Garp* he indulges in allusions to
his own previous novels when discussing his protagonist's work—like Nabokov (e.g., *Look at the Harlequins*),
he is glancing backward at his own career through
Garp. For example, Garp's first novel, *Procrastination*,
treats of a familiar historical setting, Vienna during

the years 1938 to 1945; it focuses on a young anar-
chist who frees the animals from the Schönbrunn
zoo:

> When the population of Vienna begins seriously starv-
> ing, and the midnight raids on the zoo are a common
> source of stolen food, the anarchist decides to liberate
> the remaining animals—who are, of course, innocent
> of his country's own procrastination and its acquies-
> cence to Nazi Germany. But by then the animals
> themselves are starving; when the anarchist frees them,
> they eat him.

After the Russian occupation, the boy's mother, in an
effort to awaken the complacent city, attempts another zoo break, but this, too, fails, and shortly thereafter
the mother discovers that she has cancer. In a dream
before her death, she envisions a moment of freedom: ". . . She imagines that some animals escape
from the zoo: a couple of Asiatic Black Bears. She
imagines them surviving and multiplying so successfully that they become famous as a new animal
species in the valley of the Danube."

This novel, of course, closely parallels Irving's
own *Setting Free the Bears*, which concentrates on the
same historical moment and highlights the motif of
the zoo break. Some differences in plot outline differentiate the two works, but both deal thematically with
death and the futile gesture, while concluding with
hopeful visions of freed bears. In Garp's novel this
final vision is strictly imaginary, whereas in Irving's it
reflects an actual happening—Garp's version is less
optimistic, suggesting that the desired escape can
come only through the imagination. Appropriately
enough, Garp's final word is on death: "The novel
ends—after the old woman's death—with the death
of the diarrhetic bear in the Schönbrunn zoo."

Not only *Setting Free the Bears,* but also *The 158-Pound Marriage* is made use of in this process of retrospection. Irving first mirrors the latter novel in the Garps' life: the couple's best friends are Harrison Fletcher, a colleague of Helen's at the university, and his wife Alice, a writer. Helen inaugurates a sexual exchange by sleeping with Harrison in order to help him get over a relationship with a student; Garp, then, feels authorized to have an affair with Alice. In the complex relationship that thus develops, Helen enjoys the arrangement least and calls an end to it—in this way her role corresponds to that of Severin Winter in the earlier novel. Garp then writes a novel about a sexual foursome, entitled *Second Wind of the Cuckold* (an echo of the final line of *The 158-Pound Marriage*). Again, Garp's work represents a reinterpretation of Irving's own. Rather than a studied intellectual and emotional drama like the original, his is a farce in which the central situation's realistic abnormality is exaggerated, and very likely undercut, in the portrayal of a pervasive physical defectiveness: one character is blind, one stutters, another suffers from "unstoppable flatulence," and the fourth suffers from muscle spasms.

While Irving clearly enjoys this playing with his own career, he is simultaneously making a serious point about his protagonist—Garp's vision is a limited one, consistently colored by autobiography and his obsession with death; he is unable to get beyond his personal life. Irving's actual novels surpass Garp's in scope, vision, and treatment, but by parodying them, he seems, in effect, to be discarding them as not being good enough. *The World According to Garp,* apparently, is Irving's attempt to transcend this earlier work, to achieve his own new level of artistic control.

The beginning of Garp's literary career coincides with the publication of his mother's *A Sexual Suspect.*

His books do not sell well, but Jenny's is an immediate sensation, labeled "the first truly feminist autobiography." Jenny herself is adopted as a heroine by various women's groups all over the country and considered a guru by others. Generous and ministrative by nature as well as by training, she responds to her celebrity status by taking in victims of rape and trying to help as many women as she can, although she remains uncomfortable in her role as a "feminist." After the death of her parents, Jenny even converts the estate at Dog's Head Harbor into a refuge for women.

Garp, naturally, encounters many of his mother's wards, particularly rape victims. He writes that "I feel uneasy . . . that my life has come in contact with so much rape." He becomes particularly infuriated by the Ellen Jamesians, who have cut out their tongues to protest the rape and mutilation of an eleven-year-old girl, because he considers theirs a useless and foolish gesture, a grotesque exploitation of real suffering. The Ellen Jamesians, self-mutilation, rape, and the many mangled organs thus introduced reinforce one of the novel's central concepts: the strange connection between the world of the word and the energies of sex, rape, and violence. Garp's discomfiture at his own proximity to "so much rape" is directly related to a question he asks himself later: "Why is my life so full of people with impaired speech?"—in this novel any rape of one's sensibility involves, ultimately, an inability to communicate. Garp's anger at the Ellen Jamesians is, therefore, justified, because if the perversion of sex is rape, the perversion of language is propaganda, hysteria, and other forms of voicelessness. If Irving's style becomes at times perverse, it is because his novel concerns such violent extremes, or perversions, of basic human impulses. Language and sex are related in that both are potentially creative, connective forces whose uses, however, must be tempered with some constructive restraint; both may become powerful divisive influences when misused or abused.

Nowhere is this point made clearer than in Garp's reaction to the sex-related violence of the accident in which one of his sons is killed and the other grotesquely mutilated. This, the story's central violent episode, is motivated, as in Irving's two previous novels, by infidelity. During the course of his marriage Garp has had some minor affairs with baby-sitters; in one instance he likens the seduction to a "rape-like situation." Neither this philandering, nor the *ménage à quatre* with the Fletchers, however, has greatly upset the Garps' marriage, which seems essentially a stable one. A serious rift does threaten when Helen becomes involved with a graduate student named Michael Milton; Helen agrees to end the affair when Garp learns of it. On the night his wife is to end her affair, Garp takes the children to the movies, while Helen sits with her lover in his car in the snowy driveway of the Garps' house. There, hurt and then angered by his dismissal, Milton insists on oral sex before he leaves. While this is going on, Garp and the children return, coasting blindly up the driveway in the dark. The resulting crash, graphically described, causes Helen to bite off part of Michael Milton's penis (making this scene, in effect, reminiscent of the window-sash episode of *Tristram Shandy*), breaks Garp's jaw, costs Duncan an eye, and kills Walt. It is the most devastating scene in all of Irving's fiction.

The accident and its aftermath, described in the novel's central chapter, "The World According to Marcus Aurelius," constitute Garp's most traumatic confrontation with the Under Toad; his efforts thereafter to reconcile his experience with some coherent view of the world underlie the chapter's structure and determine the rest of the novel. Like Aurelius himself, now, Garp must struggle to deal with the mayhem around him. While convalescing at Dog's Head Harbor, Garp becomes, also, a kind of Ellen Jamesian —his tongue mangled and his jaw wired shut, he cannot speak, and must communicate by writing notes. Thus forced to become like the group he hates, Garp begins his mental and emotional journey toward the sympathy, control, and tolerance that are missing from his headstrong personality. This process will take time, for Garp's failures as a person are only beginning to become apparent to him, but when his best friend, the transsexual Roberta Muldoon, tells him "there's such sympathy for people, in what you write . . . but I don't see that much sympathy in you, in your real life," Garp must accept the validity of this judgment—his mother has told him as much many times.

As was emphasized in Helen's criticism of his short story "Vigilance," a heavily autobiographical account of his own propensity for chasing down speeding cars in his neighborhood in an attempt to ensure the safety of his children—comparing it unfavorably with "The Pension Grillparzer," she commented, "One is about something and one is about nothing. . . . One is about people and one is only about you." Garp's art has tended to reflect only Garp. Trapped, imaginatively, within his private experience, Garp has suffered, like the narrator of *The 158-Pound Marriage,* from the lack of a "wide-angle" view. He does not manage easily or instantly to acquire this needed release from the suffocating narrow focus of his imagination, however—in his third novel, written in the aftermath of the accident, he confronts the shock of catastrophic loss by producing a work of a corresponding extremity of violent effect. *The World According to Bensenhaver* represents a complete surrender of purpose, a dramatic loss of creative voice as a result of his inability to feel or articulate properly the horror of his own experience. Unable to remain "pure, sane, temperate, just," or to be "sane and wholesome in your speech,"[9] as Marcus Aurelius counsels, in the expression of his grief—although he maintains a remarkable outward calm—Garp loses control of his art in a convulsive outpouring of his personal feelings of outrage, revulsion, and despair. Whereas Helen seeks wholeness through sex and procreation—at the birth of Jenny Garp, her mother "was grateful; she felt for the first time since the accident that she was delivered from the insanity of grief that had crushed her with the loss of Walt" —Garp, instead, attempts, through his art, to "buy a sort of isolation from the real and terrible world." *The World According to Bensenhaver* is a graphic and lurid reflection of the violence in Garp's world, wherein the author's darkest fears are allowed free rein in a sensational tale of rape, murder, paranoia, and guilt.

The novel begins with the rape of Hope Standish by Oren Rath and his subsequent death at her hands. Arden Bensenhaver, a policeman who has handled the case, is then hired by Hope's husband to protect his family—as Irving's narrator describes it,

> *The World According to Bensenhaver* is about the impossible desire of the husband, Dorsey Standish, to protect his wife and child from the brutal world; thus Arden Bensenhaver . . . is hired to live like an armed uncle in the house with the Standish family—he becomes the loveable family bodyguard, whom Hope must finally reject.

Bensenhaver, described as "a lurker at the last edge of light," becomes eventually the personification of the Under Toad, more a menace than a family protector; finally he kills the man whom he was hired

to protect and ends up raving mad, going "on and on
with his versions of the nightmarish world from his
wheelchair in an old age home for the criminally
insane." The narrator concludes his consideration of
the novel by recognizing the duality of response
called forth by such human calamity:

> [Bensenhaver] is seen, finally, as belonging where he is.
> Hope and her children visit him often, not merely out
> of kindness—for they are kind—but also to remind
> themselves of their own precious sanity. Hope's endur-
> ance, and the survival of her two children, make
> the old man's ravings tolerable, finally even comic to
> her.

*Bensenhaver* is a great success, making Garp independently wealthy, and like his mother's *A Sexual Suspect*,
it becomes a bible for some feminists.

   As a catharsis experience, or exorcism of his
personal grief, however, the writing of this novel
proves ineffective, its sensational plot and lurid treatment failing to bridge the gap of loss or to forward
Garp's own progress toward understanding and acceptance. Whereas all of Irving's heroes feel com-
pelled to write as a way of confronting the world and
understanding it, Garp's experience shows that self-
expression is not the only, nor always an effective
means of doing so. Loss of speech may represent a
kind of death in Irving's world, but reassertion
through language does not inevitably bring about
reconciliation. Language itself remains important if it
is used properly, not in any extreme way such as the
novel's more radical groups practice, nor in the "new
fictional" way in which language merely feeds upon
itself, but when intimately connected with action.
Garp's nightmare experience will, at last, transform him, but it is to be life itself—and yet an-

other death—rather than his art that actuates the change.

The concept of metamorphosis is central to the novel, for not only its protagonist but various characters and groups who are prominent in the story are seen to be engaged in various kinds and stages of transformation, generally sexually oriented and often extreme in nature. Most strident, and most provoking to Garp, are the Ellen Jamesians, whose obsession with rape and monstrous method of protest constitute a direct reference to the mythical tale of Philomela, recounted in Ovid's *Metamorphoses*. Raped by Tereus, her sister's husband, Philomela has her tongue cut out to forestall her revenging herself by revealing the deed. Thereafter imprisoned in a palace, she yet manages to weave her story into a tapestry and sends it to her sister, Procne. Maddened with anger, Procne then kills their son and serves the child to her husband for dinner. When Tereus, in turn, learns of this, he sets out to kill the sisters, but before he can do so, all three are turned into birds: Procne into a nightingale, Philomela into a twittering (songless) sparrow, and Tereus into an ugly hawk.[10] In the world according to Ovid, the nature of things is transformation—even out of rape may come truth and the sweetest of songbirds. In Irving's story, the horror of Ellen James's experience and the grotesque sacrifice practiced by her rabid band of avengers is to issue at last in some reconciliation with Garp the archetypal male and some new creativity in the work of Garp the artist (the nightingale was a popular symbol of the artist among the Romantic poets). Having deliberately thwarted their own facilities of communication, except through the medium of the written notes that recall Philomela's tapestry, this group, and then even Ellen James, the true victim, thus play a significant part in the transformation of the central figure in this novel about sexual strife and true liberation.

Garp's personal metamorphosis is less a matter of such direct physical mutilation than of a gradual evolution in sensibility from the sex-limited awareness of a confused, aggressive maleness to the broader vision and constructive conservatism of mature fatherhood. As befits his artistic role, in addition, this developmental progress finds clearest reflection in the writing career that parallels (and, for a time, parasitizes) his private life, demonstrating at each stage the kind and degree of his emotional adjustment.

Although he has been initiated in carnality by Cushing Percy during his prep school days, Garp receives his first conceptual introduction to sexual relations from the dying prostitute Charlotte in Vienna. There, as his real mother tries to work through her own continuing puzzlement over the phenomenon of human lust, Garp indulges first a physical, then an affectional attachment to the whore who is old enough to be his mother; indeed, the strong element of filial devotion in his infatuation is confirmed when he represents himself as Charlotte's son in order to explain his attendance at her sickbed. (There is, in this relationship, a strong echo of the popular literary motif of the naive American's confrontation with the worldy wisdom of a sophisticated European—also a facet of *The 158-Pound Marriage*—but Irving does not here press this Jamesian cultural theme beyond the sphere of his protagonist's own awareness.) Charlotte's death from a long process of internal decay—again, mirroring that of the city she typifies—only confirms his passionate absorption in the related mysteries of sex, death, and the artist's "vision." Garp's experience with the whore, culminating at her death, directly inspires the writing of "The

Pension Grillparzer," which he then uses as a means of wooing Helen. The story's morbid content and heavy symbolism thus reflect the emotional turmoil of adolescent awakening; despite its imaginative gymnastics and baroque style, "Grillparzer" is the work of a very young man, albeit a talented one. It is consumed by Garp's immature devotion to Charlotte and his concurrent desire to win Helen, and it is clouded by his unfocused sense of the deeper meanings of his rather bizarre experience—this young American has swallowed his European lesson whole, without really digesting it.

Soon thereafter, Garp returns home, marries Helen, and has his first child, but he does not yet demonstrate a true readiness for the roles of husband and father—he enjoys brief affairs with baby-sitters, and "lust" still troubles his life. Garp is yet overwhelmed by what he experiences, and unable to control his reactions either to physical temptation or to the sex-related violence around him, with which he must acknowledge a kinship. In a central episode, he encounters a molested child while jogging in the park, and in his blind desire to punish the criminal, he abuses an innocent man before catching up with the real culprit, "the Mustache Kid." Garp becomes suddenly obsessed with rape because of this incident and his simultaneous involvement with the Ellen Jamesians—it was an act "that disgusted him with himself—with his own very male instincts." He is becoming, as well, an excessively protective father; sometime later when he takes Duncan to a basketball game, he is appalled to discover that the Mustache Kid is a ticket-taker: "He knew that he wanted to hurt the Mustache Kid, on the spot—in front of Duncan. He wished he could arrange a maiming as a kind of moral lesson." This reaction is no more constructive than that of the Ellen Jamesians; nor is his misguided, though endearing, compulsion to guard Duncan from all possible harm—Duncan will later tell his father that his protectiveness has had its negative effects, and, in the end, it proves unavailing even so. Garp's desire to have a second child is, likewise, rooted in this anxiety: "He knew he was a overwatchful, worrisome father and he felt he might relieve Duncan of some of the pressure of fatherly fears if there was *another* child to absorb some of Garp's excess anxiety."

It is not surprising, then, that Garp's first novel, written shortly after his marriage, does not demonstrate a significant widening of his perspective. *Procrastination*, like "Grillparzer," is rooted in Vienna, grounded in history, and still gives death and defeat the final word. Despite Garp's ostensible maturity, his vision is still not a compelling one—his failure yet to achieve true marriage or to direct his fatherhood in a positive way is reflected in the limitation of his art. Of Dostoevsky's *The Eternal Husband,* Garp admiringly says, ". . . his characters are so complex, psychologically and emotionally; and the situations are so ambiguous." Garp's own fictions lack "ambiguity," perhaps because he himself lacks the psychological and emotional complexity of real commitment to the roles he has adopted in his own life.

Garp's second novel, *Second Wind of the Cuckold,* is also a by-product of his sexual experience—this time, of the experiment in mate swapping which the Garps undertake with the Fletchers. As Irving demonstrated in *The 158-Pound Marriage,* this, too, is a dodging of responsibility and commitment, benefiting none of the partners involved and only jeopardizing the already tenuous communication between the married couples themselves. Self-absorbed and tactless in his use of this personal adventure, Garp is not yet ready to write an honestly reflective novel, but produces instead only a slapstick farce, very much like the four-way relationship itself.

Throughout their married life, Garp and Helen have exchanged the conventional domestic roles—he cooks, cleans house, and cares for the children, while she pursues her academic career. Despite this reversal, Garp has not achieved much understanding or sympathy for women's problems—he exhibits only impatience at his mother's activities. Meeting with the troubled Mrs. Ralph, for instance, he simply condemns her as an irresponsible, inadequate mother, of concern to him only because her conduct may affect his own son. On the evening when Garp jogs over after midnight to check on Duncan, who is sleeping over at his friend's house, his fatherly fears are realized when he finds all the lights blazing, the door open, and the children sleeping in front of a noisy television set. Mrs. Ralph is having trouble with a lover upstairs, and Garp is able to help her get rid of the man, but then he himself reacts to the situation with an odd mixture of lustful feelings for the woman and anxious disapproval of her sloppy parenting. Having engaged in some pointless sexual fencing with Mrs. Ralph, also managing clumsily to arouse Helen's jealousy, he finally retreats ineffectually from the scene, dragging along with him a sleepy and confused Duncan.

Garp's weakest fiction, "Vigilance," comes after a long artistic block, and it is written to woo Helen back. Jealous of her growing interest in Michael Milton, Garp proposes to attract her attention by the seriousness of his art, as he did originally with "The Pension Grillparzer." "Vigilance," however, proves to be a limp and uninspired story; totally rooted in autobiography, it is an unimaginative rendering of Garp's own efforts to keep his neighborhood safe from speeders. It is not even successful in winning back Helen, who

resents the petulance of his attempt to extort attention and approval in this way as much as she dislikes
the narrow egoism of the story itself—she soon becomes even more deeply involved with Milton.

*The World According to Bensenhaver* is a direct
result of Garp's failure to straighten out his relationship with Helen after this episode of her infidelity
and the tragedy of Walt's death. Once again Garp's
violent reaction to an event clouds his vision and
limits his art, resulting in his most sensational (however well written) and pessimistic work. Unable to
express his personal feelings of hurt, betrayal, and
guilt—both because of the temporary speechlessness
caused by the accident and because his emotions are
choked back in the effort to treat his wife and
remaining son with an unnatural gentleness—he
pours them into the nightmare vision of this novel,
whose resulting lurid style and subject matter only
ensure its celebrity among readers who are uninter-
ested or unsympathetic to Garp's own avowed aesthetic purposes.

The turning point in Garp's metamorphosis occurs when his mother is assassinated while she is
speaking at a feminist rally. It is at her funeral that
Garp, disguised as a woman, finally learns what it is
like to be female: as a woman he is stared at, discrimi-
nated against, and even propositioned—he mutters
"Fucking men" to himself as he experiences life from
this new perspective. He even comes to a greater
understanding of the self-mutilation of the Ellen
Jamesians: ". . . Garp, now touched by the mad
women in front of him, felt the whole history of the
world's self-mutilation—though violent and illogical,
it expressed, perhaps like nothing else, a terrible
hurt."

On the airplane back to New England, Garp's
usual angry reaction is replaced by one of compassion

and sympathy, as he meets the real Ellen James, a lonely and much harassed individual, who turns out to be, ironically, an admirer of *Bensenhaver*. Suddenly, too, he comes to a real appreciation of his mother's life:

> . . . Garp finally understood what his mother's talent had been: she had right instincts—*Jenny Fields always did what was right*. One day, Garp hoped, he would see the connection between this lesson and his own writing. . . . T. S. Garp decided he would try to *be* more like his mother, Jenny Fields.

He finds himself acting upon this resolve almost immediately, when, touched by the plight of Ellen James, he promptly adopts her: "'Well, you have a family *now*,' Garp told Ellen James; he held her hand and winced to hear himself make such an offer. He heard the echo of his mother's voice, her old soap-opera role: The Adventures of Good Nurse." But Garp understands that the "Good Nurse" dealt with the world with active, helpful kindness, and he recognizes this as a more positive way of battling the Under Toad than his own frenzied, and ineffective, attempts to guard against danger of any kind.

Jenny's death is quickly followed by the deaths of Ernie Holm, Helen's father, and of Stewie Percy, an old nemesis at the Steering School—it seems one generation must pass before Garp can completely transform himself from son to father. Symbolically, he carries Stewart Percy's coffin at the funeral. The full burden of his fatherhood becomes official, soon afterward, when Garp learns that he has been named executor of Jenny's estate and must manage the charitable menage at Dog's Head Harbor. There he becomes a wise and compassionate administrator of the services provided to Jenny's extensive community of dispossessed women, and he even insists on making a public apology to the Ellen Jamesians. He then begins writing seriously again. He first collaborates with Duncan on a father-son edition of 'The Pension Grillparzer'—"its rebirth had been a rebirth for him," and then begins a new novel, entitled *My Father's Illusions:* "Because he was inventing a father, Garp felt more in touch with the spirit of pure imagination that he felt had kindled 'The Pension Grillparzer.' A long way from which he had been falsely led. . . . He felt cocky again, as if he could make up anything." For Helen, who comes out of retirement to teach at the Steering School, he becomes "the determined young Garp who made her fall in love." At the Jenny Fields Foundation he is very generous, and his family cherishes his new "good mood."

After the period of recovery and some readjustment to the needs of his expanded family, Garp's vision and his blocked imagination at last seem to open up and to be heading in the direction his talent has always promised. Once again, the change is sexually manifested, though this time the signs are positive ones—Garp and Helen are able to reaffirm their marriage by having another child, and for the first time he acts as a true father and true protector, not the anxiety-ridden protector of old, and not only of his immediate family but of women in general—his most symbolic act is adopting Ellen James. And, at last, he becomes a true husband as well: "Garp was happy with Helen. He wasn't unfaithful to her anymore; that thought seldom occurred to him." Irving's attitudes toward sex and marriage, thus embodied, are quite conservative, despite the salacious content of much of his fiction; he has little patience, really, with sexual experimentation, loud causes, and trendy solutions. Garp, finally, finds his maturity in making a total commitment to the life-affirming values of family and responsibility, and he regains control of his art when he discards clever tricks in favor of the ambiguities of felt experience.

Garp's private and artistic metamorphosis is mirrored in that of Roberta Muldoon, a former tight end for the Philadelphia Eagles, who actually changes from a man into a woman. In a sense, Roberta reclassifies herself, although throughout much of the novel the rest of the world has difficulty accepting her transformation. If the turning point in Garp's metamorphosis comes when he dresses as a woman for his mother's funeral, Robert Muldoon's comes with his sex-change operation.

Roberta is introduced as one of Jenny Fields's followers shortly after Garp meets the Ellen Jamesians; for Garp, Roberta provides a welcome contrast to that group's hysteria, and he takes an immediate liking to her. She does not appear again, however, until the aftermath of the accident. From that point on, she becomes a central figure in Garp's life—his teacher, almost a surrogate mother/father after Jenny's death. It is Roberta who takes Garp to his mother's funeral and afterwards instructs the son in his mother's legacy, impressing upon Garp the reasons for Jenny's making him her executor: ". . . this is important. Don't you see? She wanted *you* to understand the need, she wanted you to have to deal with the problems." Roberta serves, also, as a surrogate mother/father to Duncan after the accident, when Garp and Helen are too sick and grief-stricken to be effective parents. Then, after Garp's death, she becomes Duncan's closest friend, as well as Helen's.

Roberta's physical reclassification is not wholly successful; her male body is always giving her trouble, and she never completely realizes the transformation. Later in her life, this becomes particularly difficult:

> In her late fifties, she was becoming forgetful of using her estrogen, which must be used for the whole of a transsexual's life to maintain a female body shape. The lapses in her estrogen, and her stepped-up running, made Roberta's large body change shape, and change back again, before Helen's eyes.

In certain ways she is like her adopted mother, Jenny Fields, a generous and rather spiritual person who rejects the body in her dedication to the needs of others; like Jenny, she never marries. She does succeed, however, in getting rid of her killer instinct, something Irving labels as "basically male and basically intolerant," and her legacy to Garp is in helping him to overcome this impulsive aggression in himself. Thus, while her body gives her trouble, Roberta's spirit remains firm and strong, and here her metamorphosis is a triumph of true liberation.

Roberta's greatest gift, and in a sense, the most significant effect of her struggle for reclassification, comes when Duncan marries a transsexual—at least in the next generation, in life after Garp (and after Roberta) there is hope for real change, for true and lasting progress toward the goals of sexual transcendence and mutual understanding. This is perhaps Irving's most hopeful and life-affirming gesture in the novel; here he manages even to transcend Aurelius in acknowledging change, as, nodding toward Ovid, he celebrates the redemptive possibilities of metamorphosis.

"In the world according to Garp, an evening could be hilarious and the next morning could be murderous." This comment capsulizes both the nov-

el's structure and Irving's characteristic style of mix-
ing broad humor with violence and tragedy. It also
portends Garp's fate, for at the height of his artistic
development, at the moment of his fullest adjustment
to the sexual struggle that has entangled his life, he,
too, is assassinated—shot by Pooh Percy, a crazed
Ellen Jamesian who holds Garp responsible for the
death of her sister Cushy. Ironically, Garp dies in
the wrestling room, a symbol of safety and security,
the place "padded against pain," the site of his first
meeting with Helen and of Duncan's conception.
Garp's death, however, is a moment of affirmation;
he feels grateful for Helen's presence, her "scent,"
and for the odors of the wrestling room:

> Garp looked at Helen; all he could move was his
> eyes. Helen, he saw, was trying to smile back at him.
> With his eyes, Garp tried to reassure her: don't
> worry—so what if there is no life after death? There is
> life after Garp, believe me. Even if there is only death
> after death (after death), be grateful for small favors
> —sometimes there is birth after sex, for example. And,
> if you are very fortunate, sometimes there is sex after
> birth!

Herein is a strong echo of the reconciliation and
acceptance preached by his mentor, Marcus Aurelius:

> O man, citizenship of this great world-city has been
> yours. Whether for five years or five score, what is that
> to you? . . . You are not ejected from the city by any
> unjust judge or tyrant, but by the self same Nature
> which brought you into it. . . . Pass on your way, then,
> with a smiling face, under the smile of him who bids
> you go.[11]

At the end of his life and in his death, Garp tran-
scends even his mother, emerging as the true moral

center of the novel. Whereas Jenny, in pursuing her life, rejected the body, Garp does not—although heir to his mother's compassion and her energy (spirit), he remains the Garp who views sex as an act of "terrific optimism," realizing its potential in his role as a loving husband and father.

In his final chapter, "Life After Garp," Irving provides an epilogue: "'An epilogue,' Garp wrote, 'is more than a body count. An epilogue, in the disguise of wrapping up the past, is really a way of warning us about the future.'"

Here again Irving echoes Aurelius and reemphasizes his identification with the cyclical notion of history: "Reflect often how all the life of today is a repetition of the past; and observe that it also presages what is to come. . . . The performance is always the same; it is only the actors who change.[12]

Life after Garp, conditioned by death, turns out to be much the same as life before and during Garp. The important thing, however, is that Garp's energy, his life and its meaning, continue to affect his family: Duncan, Helen, and Jenny become closer, and learn to lead productive lives. The epilogue, despite its emphasis on body counts, thus concludes the story with a sense not of death but of life. The final note singles out Jenny Garp, who combines the best qualities of her forebears: having become a doctor, specializing in cancer treatment, she, like her father, sees only "terminal cases"; like her mother, she is a "brilliant student"; and like her grandmother, she is an independent woman, a healer, and a "roamer of hospitals." Jenny provides, finally, some proof of progress in the sexual revolution that has animated the whole history of her family in the complete, and seemingly effortless, liberation from sexual role that her brief biography suggests. Unlike Jenny Fields, "Good Nurse" and self-proclaimed "sexual suspect,"

Jenny Garp becomes a doctor—indeed, a researcher rather than a clinician—and seems to achieve, in her second marriage, a successful blending of sexuality and selfhood. The anguished struggle of the interim generation—Garp's emotional metamorphosis and Helen's awkward search for personal fulfillment— seem thus to be smoothly resolved in the life of this child of their ultimate crisis.

Despite its multiple thematic threads, *The World According to Garp* is essentially a family story, and its appeal on that level is what made it such an outstanding popular success. What is most memorable about Jenny, Garp, and Helen is their complex interaction as a family, in their roles as mother, son, husband, father, and wife. Greil Marcus points out that in the novel,

> Irving was able to combine horror with domesticity without compromising the reality of either. He did not imply, as is the American way, that because domesticity (or whatever) can contain horror, domesticity itself is horrible—or horror a germ that can be stamped out with the right moral vaccine. He was able to take something of the aesthetics of literary "black comedy" out of their arty, comic-book world and interweave them with the mundane and the recognizable. . . .[13]

When Irving writes that "in the world according to Garp we are all terminal cases," the seeming simplicity of the statement reflects not upon the carnage that has preceded it but upon the power of its author's optimism, for the novel which it concludes stands, finally, as a vital exemplar of what is perhaps the central statement of Aurelius's *Meditations:*

> If you do the task before you always adhering to strict reason with zeal and energy and yet with humanity, disregarding all lesser ends and keeping the divinity

within you pure and upright, as though you were even now faced with its recall—if you hold steadily to this, staying for nothing and shrinking from nothing, only seeking in each passing action a conformity with nature and in each word and utterance a fierce truthfulness, then shall the good life be yours. And from this course no man has the power to hold you back.[14]

# CHAPTER 6

# My Father's Illusions

Near the end of *The World According to Garp,* Garp, in an expansive and creative frame of mind, announces ideas for some forthcoming novels. The first of these is entitled *My Father's Illusions,* and Garp describes the plot in part:

> It's about an idealistic father who has many children. He keeps establishing little utopias for his kids to grow up in, and after his kids grow up he becomes a founder of small colleges. But all of them go broke—the colleges and the kids. . . . Meanwhile, his wife divorces him and his children keep growing older, and turning out unhappy, or fucked up—or just perfectly normal, you know. The only thing the children have in common are these dreadful memories of the utopias their father tried to have them grow up in.

Like Garp's other novels that resemble Irving's own, this one shares only some surface similarities with Irving's fifth novel, *The Hotel New Hampshire.* This work does, indeed, introduce an idealistic father of five, who would seem to be seeking "little utopias" for his children—the utopias are hotels—but that is about where the similarities end, although "My Father's

Illusions" might serve as an appropriate subtitle for Irving's novel.

At first glance, it appears that Irving is once more mining the same material that he exploited in the earlier fiction. Again, bears appear as symbols, there is the inevitable trip to Vienna, the American setting is an academic community, and the forces of death and violence are pervasive. Despite such superficial echoes, however, *The Hotel New Hampshire* represents a marked departure from the fictional method of Irving's previous work. Some familiar motifs are discoverable, but they are used differently. No longer merely symbolic, bears become major characters here; Vienna still is a place where the protagonists mature, but the historical focus has shifted from mid-twentieth century to its *fin de siècle* culture; and this novel's violence is decidedly less horrific, less brutal, lacking the emotional punch that is characteristic of the previous novels. The nuclear family remains Irving's focus, though here it is the family unit itself, rather than any single protagonist, which dominates the narrative action. By the story's end, the narrator, John, has become the novel's moral center, but his fate remains inextricably bound up with that of his parents and his siblings.

The most extreme departure, however, is in the form of the work itself. Irving has previously operated within the parameters of the traditional novel; as has been pointed out, he is much concerned with narrative structure and movement, with the development of character, and certainly with the creation of a definable universe in which all aspects of his tale take on life, shape, and function. His art has not been strictly mimetic—his situations and characters are frequently too exaggerated, becoming grotesque as he stretches reality in order to dramatize its essence.

Irving's accomplishment as a writer has always been
that despite his excesses, his world is easily identifiable as our own; his characters are psychologically true
and their relationships and motivations are accurate
and penetrating. Their psychological and moral
growth (or lack of it) has been traceable throughout
each novel.

The Hotel New Hampshire is a more symbolic novel,
portraying a much more insular and hermetic world
than the others. Little attention is paid to describing
its various locales; even Vienna, easily the most vital
place in the earlier works, is left sketchy here. Also,
the characters, however well developed, are less
three-dimensional individuals than emblematic figures, formally arranged and representative of symp-
toms, states of mind, or stages of emotional development. Here Irving is very much in the tradition of the
classic American novel, where character and setting
take a back seat to the exploration of metaphysical
states or philosophic dilemmas.

This novel can best be described as a kind of
fairy tale, and the narrator often refers to it as such.
Its basic method corresponds closely to what Bruno
Bettelheim has defined as the characteristic mode of
fairy-tale narrative:

> In a fairy tale, internal processes are externalized and
> become comprehensible as represented by figures of
> the story and its events. . . . The unrealistic nature of
> these tales is an important device, because it makes
> obvious that the fairy tales' concern is not useful
> information about the external world, but the inner
> processes taking place in the individual.[1]

Like a fairy tale, The Hotel New Hampshire is essentially
a childhood story, basically concerned with children

and their growing up. Unlike *Garp,* it does not follow most of the characters through their whole lives; rather, the novel concentrates on the maturation process, pursuing its characters only to the threshold of adulthood, highlighting the experiences and the discovery of identity necessary to the attainment of that state. Like all of Irving's novels, *Hotel* reflects much violence and adversity, but like *Garp,* and like all fairy tales, its narrative insists that a rewarding and fulfilling life is within one's grasp despite great hardship. The Under Toad, here taking the shape of a stuffed dog named Sorrow, is once again pervasive, and Irving insists anew on the need to recognize and understand it, and so, perhaps, to neutralize its power. Thus, he suggests, one may achieve a true and lasting identity, establishing a strong personality in the struggle against the impersonal forces of death and destruction which menace this life. Bettelheim argues for the fairy tale's function as a major agent in a child's socialization process; this same agency is a primary function of *The Hotel New Hampshire,* whose imaginative artistry, however, is addressed to an adult audience that is presumably as much in need of caution and comfort as any child confronting the world.

The basic outlines of the plot are simple and can be divided into three parts corresponding to the family's successive hotel environments. The story opens with the courtship and marriage of Winslow (Win) and Mary Berry and the birth of their five children. The family lives in Dairy, New Hampshire, where Father first teaches English at the Dairy School, a second-rate private school, and later opens the first Hotel New Hampshire. The children live a relatively happy life there, the three eldest, Frank, Franny, and John, all attending the Dairy School. The most troubling event of this period is Franny's rape at the age of fifteen. Later, at the invitation of Father's former mentor, a Viennese Jew and bear trainer named Freud, the family travels to Vienna to help run a hotel there—the second Hotel New Hampshire. En route to Vienna, Mother and Egg, the youngest child, are killed in a plane crash. In Vienna, the Berrys become involved with a group of tawdry prostitutes and a motley band of revolutionaries, who together comprise a variety of human grotesquerie as symbolically vivid as any fairy tale's register of fabulous beasts. This part of the novel culminates when the family and Freud avert the revolutionaries' attempt to blow up the Vienna Opera House; Freud is killed and Father is blinded during the skirmish. The final part of the novel brings the family back to America, heroes and wealthy. The plot then concludes with younger sister Lilly's suicide (brought on by the pressures of her authorship), after which the surviving family members finally manage to adjust happily. John, now married, cares for his father at the third Hotel New Hampshire, a rape crisis center run by his wife; Franny has become a famous actress, married to her childhood sweetheart; and Frank has become a wealthy agent.

Bettelheim writes that the fairy tale answers the eternal questions: "What is the world really like? How am I to live my life in it? How can I truly be myself?"[2] The answers to these questions, he emphasizes, are implied and suggested, never spelled out: "Fairy tales leave to the child's fantasizing whether and how to apply to himself what the story reveals about life and human nature."[3] Irving has dealt with these three central questions in all of his novels, but in *Hotel* he addresses them most directly, and having forcefully confronted the world in his art, he goes on, in the

manner of fairy tales, to suggest strategies for coping
with life, and to indicate the possibilities of success in
the struggle for selfhood.

The form and content of the fairy tale conform
to the way a child views an experience of the world.
One of the most important measures of the order of
the world is projected in the image of parents and in
the makeup and dynamics of the family unit. In
commenting on *Garp,* Irving said:

> . . . I think that one of the reasons Garp and his
> family . . . have a special quality is that I haven't done
> anything with their surroundings. It is as if they live in
> a world of their own, which is, to me, just an exaggera-
> tion of what family life is like. If you live committedly
> with a family, it really is as if there is the world of your
> home and the world out there. I just carried that one
> more step by making the world out there shadowy and
> ominous.[4]

Although *Hotel* is essentially a family novel, the first
part is the only section wherein the entire family lives
together before death claims three of its members.
The three hotels function symbolically in the novel to
correspond to the various stages in the education and
evolution of the family and the narrator. The first
hotel serves as a protective, womblike place, a haven
where the children feel comfortable and secure from
the dangers of a cold, lonely world outside. Sigmund
Freud, whose presence hovers around the edge of the
novel, wrote that, ". . . the dwelling house was a
substitute for the mother's womb, the first lodging,
for which in all likelihood man still longs, and in
which he was safe and felt at ease."[5]

The other two sections of the novel, which feature the other two hotels, proceed symbolically as
well. They closely resemble the stages of what Joseph

Campbell labels the central "monomyth" that is the basic structural model of both the myth and the fairy tale: "The standard path of the mythological adventure of the hero is a magnification of the formula represented in the rites of passage: *separation— initiation—return*. . . ."[6] Whereas the family's tenure at the first Hotel New Hampshire ends with a separation, the second, in Vienna, becomes, for those who survive the journey to it, a place of initiation (Vienna functions in a similar way in all the novels). The final hotel, in a deserted area of Maine, is the site of the return, the place where the narrator/hero is able to come to grips with what he has experienced and to pass on its lessons to his readers.

*Hotel* is narrated in the first person by the third child, John (who was born in 1942, the year of John Irving's own birth). Bettelheim points out that "when the hero of a fairy tale is not an only child but one of several . . . he is nearly always the third child"[7] and he explains the significance of the number three in the following way:

> In the child's mind, "two" stands usually for the two parents, and "three" for the child himself in relation to his parents, but not to his siblings. That is why, whatever the child's position within the sibship, the number three refers to himself. When in a fairy story a child is the third one, the hearer easily identifies with him because within the most basic family constellation the child is third down, irrespective of whether he is the oldest, middle, or youngest among his siblings.
>
> Only in comparison to the parents does it make sense that "the third", meaning the child, is at the beginning so incompetent or lazy, a simpleton; and only in regard to them does he catch up so magnificently as he grows up. The child can do so only if he is

helped, taught, and promoted by an older person; as
the child may reach or surpass the parents' level
through the help of an adult teacher.[8]

John is not really a simpleton, but he does not think
highly of himself and often alludes to the fact that he
needs to grow up. He is helped along the way by
various teachers and does by the end of the novel
surpass his father.

The narration begins with the parents' courtship,
in a world of the narrator's imagination, a world of
romance and magic, where bears ride on motorcycles. It begins in a kind of "once upon a time" spirit:
"The summer my father bought the bear, none of us
was born—we weren't even conceived. . . ." John then
establishes his position as the third child and his role
as narrator:

> And so it's up to me—the middle child, and the least
> opinionated—to set the record straight, or nearly
> straight. We were a family whose favorite story was the
> story of my mother and father's romance: how Father
> bought the bear, how Mother and Father fell in love
> and had, in rapid succession, Frank, Franny, and me
> ("Bang, Bang, Bang!" as Franny would say); and, after
> a brief rest, how they then had Lilly and Egg.

For Irving, the story of the parents' courtship is a
quintessential example of the storyteller's art, because
the narrator is able, in recounting it, to embroider the
basic facts with imagination. John admits:

> I tend to see my parents in those years more clearly
> than I see them in the years I actually can remember,
> because those times I was present, of course, are
> colored by the fact that they were up-and-down times
> —about which I have up-and-down opinions. Toward

the famous summer of the bear, and the magic of my
mother and father's courtship, I can allow myself a
more consistent point of view.

The father confirms this when he says to the children,
"You imagine the story better than I remember it."
The first chapter is the most intricate and beautifully
written in the novel, as if Irving, through his narrator, is emphasizing the importance of the imagination
and the need to use it in the interpretation of
everyday life—the truth of fairy tales, Bettelheim
points out, "is the truth of our imagination."[9] This is
why the story of the parents' courtship is the favorite
story, and this is why the narrative opens with it, for
we are being placed inside the true world of the story,
the world of the imagination, where anything can
happen.

Although the narrator does mention his parents'
names, Mary Bates and Winslow Berry (Winslow is
John Irving's own middle name), these specifics are
referred to only in passing, as throughout the entire
narrative they are referred to as Mother and Father.
This, again, is in keeping with the technique of fairy
tales, where "the parents of the main figures . . .
remain nameless,"[10] facilitating the identification
process for the reader. Furthermore, the homely
allusiveness of the family name, Berry, and the name
of their hometown, Dairy, New Hampshire, sets a
tone of earthy universality, orienting the tale in the
realm of domestic archetype (cf. Cinderella, Jack and
the Beanstalk).

Both parents are children of faculty members at
the Dairy School: Mother's father was a Latin teacher,
and Father's father, Coach Bob, the football coach
(like Ernie Holm in *Garp*, Coach Bob is a widower
who comes to the Dairy School primarily so that his
son can get a good free education when he comes of

age). Having known each other only casually before-
hand, Father and Mother begin their courtship during the summer of their high school graduation at the
Arbuthnot-by-the-Sea, a resort hotel on the Maine
coast, where both are working. Father will always
associate romance with hotels because of this experience.

The summer at the Arbuthnot is described as
idyllic. The place too, seems a kind of never-
neverland, somehow divorced from the world of
concrete reality. Late in the novel, the owner of the
hotel describes Maine, and though he displays no
poetic appreciation of its remoteness, Irving's point is
made:

> "I mean, don't you know where *Maine* is? It's nowhere!
> There's no decent train service, and there's no decent
> flying service. It's a terrible place to drive to—it's too
> far from *both* New York and Boston—and when you *do*
> get there, the water's too cold and the bugs can bleed
> you to death in an hour."

Father, as the hero of this inset tale, is described as a
plausibly romantic figure:

> She'd never noticed what a handsome boy he was,
> really; he had a body as hard as Coach Bob's, but the
> Dairy School had exposed him to the manners, the
> dress, and the way with his hair that Bostonians (not
> Iowans) were favoring. He looked as if he already went
> to Harvard, whatever that must have meant to my
> mother then. . . . "He had the darkest, brightest eyes,
> and whenever you looked at him you were sure he'd
> just been looking at you—but you could never catch
> him."

And Mother, who is enjoying a final summer
fling before settling down to the task of caring

for her aging parents, seems like a maiden in distress:

> She wore white gloves and a white hat with a veil; she was dressed for "serving" at the first lawn party, and my father admired how nicely her hair hugged her head—it was longer in back, swept away from her face, and clamped somehow to the hat and veil in a manner both so simple and mysterious that my father fell to wondering about her.
> "What are you doing in the fall?" he asked her.
> Again she shrugged, but maybe my father saw in her eyes, through her white veil, that my mother was hoping to be rescued from the scenario she imagined was her future.

The other significant happening of that summer is Father's meeting Freud and his bear, State o' Maine, who entertain the guests at the hotel. When Father and Mother first see the bear dance, the moment is a magical one:

> My mother and father saw the bear begin to dance. He danced away from Freud on his hind legs; he dropped to all fours and did a short lap or two around the motorcycle. Freud stood on the motorcycle and clapped. The bear called State o' Maine began to clap, too. When my mother felt my father take her hand into his—they were not clapping—she did not resist him; she gave back equal pressure, both of them never taking their eyes from the bulky bear performing below them, and my mother thought: I am nineteen and my life is just beginning.

Animals in fairy tales usually stand for the id, or animal nature, in (Sigmund) Freudian terms. This has been the case in Irving's fiction as well, the bears,

especially in *Setting Free the Bears,* representing the
wilder, more aggressive aspects of personality. Again,
Irving has always written about bears in captivity, in
unnatural environments, either in zoos *(Setting Free
the Bears)* or in hotels ("The Pension Grillparzer"),
suggesting thus that modern society has stifled man's
basic instincts and drives. In the novel the bear is
domesticated and lives in an unnatural environment
—as Father says, "He was too old to be a bear
anymore." But Mother and Father recognize in the
bear's playful spirit their own instinctual selves, and
in that moment their love is consummated, even
though on that first night, "they didn't even kiss." It is
on that night that Father, a dreamer, truly begins to
dream:

> And what must my Father have imagined, reaching
> for her hand just because a bear was brought by a
> lobster boat into his life?
> "I knew it would be *my* bear," Father told us. "I
> don't know how." And perhaps it was this knowledge—
> that he saw something that would be his—that made
> him reach for my mother, too.

Freud—"our Freud," as the children call him in
order to distinguish him from "the other Freud,"
whose works provide a kind of external gloss on the
events of this novel—functions as a kind of supernat-
ural helper who appears to aid the hero at the outset
of his adventures. (In the imagination of his children,
Father is a hero, certainly the hero of the first
chapter's family romance; as the rest of the novel
makes clear, however, he is an unsuccessful exemplar,
unable to fulfill the hero's destiny.) Joseph Campbell
points out that in the fairy tale, when the hero is
masculine, "it may be some little fellow of the wood,

some wizard, hermit, shepherd, or smith, who appears to supply the amulets and advice that the hero
will require."[11] Irving's Freud—described upon his
appearance as "a grizzled Viennese Jew with a limp
and an unpronounceable name"—does, indeed,
come to the hotel from the woods, where he has lived
with lumberjacks and served as a mechanic and
sometime doctor. From those woods he brings with
him State o' Maine, the bear (amulet), which he will
pass on to Father along with some explicit advice
before disappearing from the story for a time.
Freud's wizardlike status is apparently confirmed by
his experience as an animal trainer and by his Viennese origin, which suggests that he has the wisdom and mystery of the Old World at his disposal—
in fact, subsequent events will prove that neither
of these qualifications can provide much magic,
for Freud never has much success with his bears,
and he himself is soon to be victimized by the irrational horror that has taken over his exotic home-
land.

In addition to seeing the bear dance and realizing that their lives are just beginning, Mother and
Father witness another vision when, later that same
night, they walk down to the docks to watch the
water. Along the dark coast, a white sloop sails toward
them and out of it steps "the man in the white dinner
jacket"—Father finds out later from Freud that this is
the owner of the hotel. Asking if Freud and the bear
have arrived, the man remarks, "Freud's a Jew, you
know. . . . It's a good thing he got out of Europe
when he did, you know. Europe's going to be no place
for Jews." A few minutes later, adds, "And the *world's*
going to be no place for *bears!*" He says something else
as he is leaving, but "what the man in the white dinner
jacket last called to them was lost in the sputter of the

engine. . . . All his life my father wished he'd heard what the man had to say."

The function of the man in the white dinner jacket can also be explained by Campbell:

> With the personifications of his destiny to guide and aid him, the hero goes forward in his adventure until he comes to the "threshold guardian" at the entrance to the zone of magnified power. Such custodians bound the world in four directions . . . standing for the limits of the hero's present sphere, or life horizon. Beyond them is darkness, the unknown, and danger. . . .[12]

Water, from where Irving's mysterious messenger comes, is one of the regions of the unknown that are, in Campbell's scheme, "free fields for the projection of unconscious content. Incestuous *libido* and patricidal *destrudo* are thence reflected back against the individual and his society in forms suggesting threats of violence. . . ."[13] One of the three elements in which life unfolds (land and sky are the others), water also evokes the womb and the beginnings of the evolutionary process. Bettelheim writes that the frog is associated with water and the id, thus a representative of the earliest evolutionary stages[14] (interesting in light of Irving's use of the Under Toad in *Garp* as the symbol of death and destruction). There could be no more profound example of the unleashed and unrestrained id than the destruction of the Jews, foretold by the man in the white dinner jacket, Irving's emissary from the unconscious, "threshold guardian" of the psychic, watery depths that the imperfect hero of this first tale will never manage to explore. This man's cryptic warnings, are thus unavailing, even partially unheard by Father's generation. As discussed in

Chapter 2, World War II, with its prologue and epilogue, represents the beginning of the post-modern world—clearly one not fit for bears, which for Irving represent not the unrestricted id, but, rather, man's natural energy, the id made to serve the best interests of the integrated personality.

The man in the white dinner jacket represents death and the underside of Father's world of dream and romance, although Father himself will never understand this: ". . . the world for my father, in the summer of '39, was new and affectionate with my mother's shy touches, the roar of the '37 Indian and the strong smell of State o' Maine; the cold Maine nights and the wisdom of Freud." In this juxta-position of scenes Irving stresses the relationship of love and death, a subject that is at the heart of all his novels (especially *Garp*) and at the center of his world. The relation of Eros and Thanatos is one of the cornerstones of Sigmund Freud's theories as well, as he argues in *Civilization and Its Discontents*:

> And now, I think, the meaning of the evolution of civilization is no longer obscure to us. It must present the struggle between Eros and Death, between the instinct of life and the instinct of destruction, as it works itself out in the human species. This struggle is what all life essentially consists of. . . .[15]

This concept underlies Irving's art as well, and is further enforced as this novel develops.

Father's failure to recognize this malignant aspect of the man in the white dinner jacket is demonstrated by his continuing to associate him with elegance, style, and his own romantic vision of the world as determined by that summer in Maine. The inability to differentiate between illusion and reality links Father with Fitzgerald's Gatsby, and the parallel is made by Irving later in the novel when the children are listening to a reading of *The Great Gatsby*, and suddenly, Lilly cries out, "Father is a *Gatsby*": "'. . . it's the man in the white dinner jacket, it's Father, he's a Gatsby . . . Don't you *see?*' she shrieked. 'There's always going to be an *It*—and *It* is going to elude us every time. It's going to *always* get away. . . . And Father's not going to stop."

Father does indeed seem to share Gatsby's rather mystical faith in life, the mesmerizing optimism that transforms the vague promise of "the American dream" into a stubborn and motivating conviction of reality. (Father's personal version of the American dream is involved in his belief that the Arbuthnot-by-the-Sea failed because "it was not democratic enough," and in his successive doomed attempts to run his own hotels "democratically.") Like Gatsby's dream, Father's proves to be a blinding (quite literally in his case) dream-vision—it is the very essence of the romantic American vision that it lacks the power of discrimination. However, again like Gatsby and other heroes of American literature, Father manages to invest his illusion with a certain grand faith, a combined sense of aspiration and destiny, which makes of the dreamer himself a kind of heroic character. This is why Gatsby remains a heroic figure, why Nick Carraway can say, "There's something gorgeous about him." And this is why, despite his failures, Father remains a hero to his children. He is an archetypal American hero in his quixotic attempts to believe in a brilliant future. As the Viennese revolutionary who reads to the children points out, "'The single ingredient in American literature that distinguishes it from other literatures of the world is a kind of giddy, illogical hopefulness. It is quite technically sophisticated while remaining ideologically naive.'"

Father spends the summer with Mother, Freud, and the bear, immersed in the dream world that will never afterwards release him. Freud, however, after meeting with an anti-Semitic German at the hotel, decides that he must return to Europe. Before he leaves, he sells the bear, now renamed Earl, to Father, and, having thus delivered the animal charm to the tale's hero, completes his wizardlike function by providing the words of guidance to lead along the path of adventure. Freud's magical advice consists of a demand for three promises. First, Father and Mother are to marry promptly—like his namesake, he realizes that these young people have not blundered accidentally into the Arbuthnot-by-the-Sea (Sigmund Freud argues that blunders are not happenstance, but the result of suppressed wishes). Second, Father must go to Harvard, where he has already been accepted. Finally, Freud warns that Mother must "forgive" Father—recognizing perhaps, that the man's dreams and illusions will cause difficulties for his wife. The three promises introduce a familiar fairy-tale motif, which is to be further elaborated in Irving's novel with recurrences of the number three. Bettelheim explains that three is a popular number in fairy tales, representing the three aspects of the mind: id, ego, and superego[16]—those aspects which must be integrated to form the whole, mature personality. Whereas the marriage and the Harvard education will provide for the young man's id-directed sexual nature and his ego-centered intellectual development, the stipulation of Mother's forgiveness represents Freud's knowledge that Father's superego will never fully develop and that Mother will have to serve in that capacity for him. She will be needed not as an agent to torment him with feelings of anxiety, but as one who comforts him and continues to protect him from the external world. And, as Freud rightly points out, "this will cost" her.

Following Freud's departure, Father and Mother return to Dairy and get married. Father then goes on the road with the bear, entertaining at various hotels up and down the East coast. During this time three of the children are born; also at this time, Father enters Harvard. His studies are interrupted by World War II, but he returns to Harvard and graduates after the war. By this time Earl is too old to perform any more, and so Father gets a job teaching English at the Dairy School.

The chapter concludes in the fall of 1946, with the family's trip to the Arbuthnot-by-the-Sea. There they find that Father and Mother's fairy-tale world is a ruin: "Bleached colorless as bones, the building stood abandoned and boarded-up; every window that was showing had been smashed or shot out." The world as Father and Mother remembered it is no more, and its demise is rendered symbolically when Earl, now practically blind, is shot by a local boy. Father breaks down and cries for his vanished dream world, which he will, however, never be able to leave behind:

> He sat beside Earl on the dock and raised the dead bear's head into his lap; he hugged Earl's old face to his stomach and cried and cried. He was crying for more than Earl, of course. He was crying for the Arbuthnot, and Freud, and for the summer of '39. . . .

The narrator's own reflections are significant:

> I was four, and I sincerely believe that this is my first memory of life itself—as opposed to what I was *told*

happened, as opposed to the pictures other people have painted for me. The man with the strong body and the gentleman's face was my father, who had come to live with us; he sat sobbing with Earl in his arms—on a rotting dock, over dangerous water. . . . My mother hugged us to her, as tightly as Father held fast to Earl.

John's first real memory, thus, is one of loss. His father—a stranger to the children since he has always been away, on the road or at school—mourns the corpse of his illusions, forever oblivious of the precariousness of his position and to the danger nearby. Mother can only comfort the children, while Father clutches at his dreams, unable to let go.

From the second chapter on, the parents fade into the background of the story and the children take center stage. The title of this transition chapter is "The First Hotel New Hampshire," and although the family does not move into it until the fourth chapter, the hotel now becomes the focal point of their existence. This first hotel, as has been pointed out, serves as a haven for the children, a secure place where they are able to take root, develop, and establish the personality traits that will distinguish them later— when the hotel officially opens, this sheltering function is announced by Iowa Bob, the grandfather: "At the Hotel New Hampshire . . . when the shit hits the fan, nobody gets blown away." Formerly the Thompson Female Seminary, which was put out of business when the Dairy School admitted women, this hotel remains a curious amalgam of childish fixtures (schoolroom chairs that are "screwed down for life," and tiny toilets) and improvised accommodation for the burgeoning family that principally inhabits it. Converting a school into a hotel is a dreadful idea, as

Mother points out, for, like old Arbuthnot's description of Maine, Dairy is a "nowhere" place:

> . . . That the town was so motley, and no one else had dreamed of putting up a place to stay in it, didn't worry my father. In New Hampshire the summer tourists went to the beaches—they were half an hour away. The mountains were an hour away, where the skiers went, and where there were summer lakes. But Dairy was valley land. . . . Dairy was close enough to the sea to feel the sea's dampness but far enough away from the sea to benefit not in the slightest from the sea's freshness.

But Mother's prudence is no match for Father's visionary will, and in the narrator's imagination, the night Father convinces Mother to help him with the hotel is bathed in romance: "Remember: it was night, and the night inspired my father. He had first seen Freud and his bear at night; he had fished with State 'o Maine at night; nighttime was the only time the man in the white dinner jacket made an appearance. . . ."

Father's dream of a hotel is, of course, an illusion, and, as is made clear by this reference to the messenger of death, it is an illusion that promises danger for the family that pursues it. John remarks, ". . . the first of my father's illusions was that bears could survive the life lived by human beings, and the second was that human beings could survive a life led in hotels."

In the world of John Irving no one is ever truly safe, and so, despite the comforting aura of this first home-hotel, the Berry children, now the protagonists of the fairy-tale adventure imposed upon them by their father's persistent dreaming, will have to confront, even here, the threatening external world of life and the Under Toad; the man in the white dinner jacket will make an occasional appearance. Their learning begins with sex and violence, initiatory aspects of Eros and Thanatos. The children are characterized almost exclusively by their sexual interests and activities: Frank, the oldest, is described by John as asocial, surly, and prudish; it is revealed early in the novel that he is homosexual. Franny is the most independent and opinionated of the children, cursing continually and dealing aggressively with the boys, whereas John's sole trait seems to be his jealous and protective love for this sister. Lilly and Egg are small children who do not figure actively in the early part of the novel.

Sequentially differentiated and varied in their adolescent sexual and preadolescent asexual orientations, this family of five siblings clearly represents a sexual spectrum, and this schematic function is reinforced by their names. Bettelheim points out that in fairy tales if children have names at all, they are very common ones, making them stand for any boy or any girl.[17] The children who figure most prominently in this Irving-esque fairy tale do indeed have common names, as is reflected in the derivation of their names: Frank is so called because his parents decide to always be frank with each other; "Franny" simply sounds like "Frank;" and John is named after John Harvard. Lilly, whose name is explicitly denied explanation, and Egg, whose actual namelessness foreshadows his childhood death—he never really progresses beyond the point of being the "baby of the family," and so requires no individualizing name—are the two siblings who will not survive the fairy-tale struggle to grow up. Like outgrown stages of the self, Lilly and Egg will be left behind as the others continue to mature. John, the protagonist/narrator (and Irving persona) concentrates on Frank and Franny, the two older siblings (and possible parent-substitutes in Bettelheim's three-member family unit) whose violently opposed personalities and counterpoint sexual development present him with dramatically divergent role models.

The children's explicitly sexual escapades always involve Franny. All are violent confrontations, and all are associated with either death or excrement, or both. On three different occasions Franny attacks or defends herself by grabbing the testicles of an older boy, causing him to cringe and groan in a way that is described as deathlike. The description of her third victim's reaction is most graphic: "She made her usual, unbeatable move for the private parts of Chipper Dove and he made the sickly motions of quitting this life forever." Chipper, the quarterback of the football team, is attacked for abusing Frank: he and some teammates, taunting Frank for his homosexuality, have been holding him splayed out over a mud puddle, immersing his genitals in the mud. Earlier, Franny had used the same tactic on Frank himself in retaliation for his grabbing her breast during a family squabble, and then, again, on Ralph De Meo, another football player, for roughing up John.

All three cases are also associated with excretion. After the incident with De Meo, Franny and John, hiding in the ferns of the forest, watch as one of the football players defecates in the woods (apparently a common practice among the members of the team). They themselves then do likewise in setting up a prank, and the incidents that follow lead to her fight with Frank. Then, after Frank, Franny, and John beat up Chipper Dove, John fills Chipper's football helmet with mud, and Franny remarks, "Shit and death." This is a reference to the school colors of the Dairy School: "Grey like the pallor of a dead man's face . . . and brown . . . like manure." Thus, in the trio's adolescent experience, sexual violence, excretion, and death are linked.

These three incidents (again the number three seems formulaic) are prologue to the rape of Franny. On Halloween night, John and Franny, hurrying through the schoolground's woods, find themselves caught up in a net, trapped with some trick-or-treaters, a prank set up by some of the football players. When their leader, Chipper Dove, discovers that Franny is one of his victims, he and two of his friends take her off into the woods and gang-rape her. John, with the help of some of the black football players, headed by the bearlike Junior Jones, attempts to rescue her, but they are too late. They are able, however, to capture two of the boys; Chipper Dove eludes them, though all three are eventually expelled from school. In the manner of a fairy tale, wherein the villians must be punished, Irving then provides a quick glimpse into the future, revealing that the two subordinates are both to die violent deaths in the company of prostitutes. Chipper Dove's fate is saved for later in the novel.

On the night of Franny's rape, there are two deaths. Patrolman Tuck suffers a heart attack on the grounds of the hotel (he is a victim of Franny's own Halloween prank), and the family dog, Sorrow, is put to sleep. Sorrow, who smelled bad, defecated on the floor, and farted uncontrollably, now becomes the controlling symbol uniting the elements of sex, excrement, and death. In discussing the function of dogs in a fairy tale entitled "The Three Languages," Bettelheim makes a useful point about man's relationship with dogs: "Dogs are the animals living in closest proximity to man. They are the animals which to the child seem most like man, but they also represent instinctual freedom—freedom to bite, to excrete in an uncontrolled way, and to indulge sexual needs without restraint. . . ."[18] Sorrow, who assumes in this novel the role of the Under Toad, was a dog who could not control his instinctual nature; in Irving's universe, the failure to harness such urges, to control and understand them, leads inevitably to death. In this tale of growing up, it is necessary for the children to confront the baser aspects of themselves and others. Only by facing the unpleasantness that Sorrow represents—and later, the omnipresent specter of death which the old dog becomes when stuffed and posed as a keepsake—will they be able eventually to understand and control it.

The confrontation with the darker aspects of the self is emphasized by the fact that most of these sex/death/excretion incidents take place in the woods. In many fairy tales the forest is a place where the central characters get lost, having been deprived of the organized life supervised by their parents. It also symbolizes the dark, hidden world of the unconscious, where sometimes anxieties and sometimes wishes are to be encountered. Franny's rape is certainly a horrific experience, a violent way for a young girl, even a sexual tease like Franny, to be introduced to sex. For John, whose one true love is his sister, the rape can be seen as a projection of his own (so far suppressed) desire to have sex with Franny. Most important, however, the experiences in the forest are projections of basic id-inspired drives, instincts uncontrolled and base, that must be overcome if they are not to lead to death.

Franny seems to take her rape in stride, her independent, strong nature apparently asserting itself in her moment of need. (Later its more severe effects on her personality will surface.) She insists that

the rapists did not get at the essential part of herself,
"the *me* in me." The aftereffects of the rape are most
apparent in Franny's need to take *three* baths a day.
Only when she overhears her parents making love in
Room *3E* of the hotel does she first begin to appreciate the nature of true, love-directed sexuality:

> "God!" Franny said. "They really *love* each other—they
> really *do!*" And I wondered why I had taken such a
> thing for granted, and why it seemed to surprise my
> sister so much. Franny dropped my hand and wrapped
> her arms around herself; she hugged herself, as if she
> was trying to wake herself up, or get warm.

After this revelation, Franny stops her obsessive
bathing and is able to look ahead to a more promising
future. Within the warm and loving confines of the
home/hotel, childhood traumas can still be eased.

This hotel is a place where the children are
allowed to be themselves. They seem almost free
from parental supervision, though they are comforted by their parents' love and presence. The hotel, too,
is part of the fairy-tale landscape—again, more a
psychological place than a real one, though a much
safer and more familiar place than the forest, which is
dark and terrifying. Frank's homosexuality goes un-
detected at home, at least by Father, and no one there
really bothers him about it; he is left free to indulge
his fondness for uniforms and his interest in taxider-
my. Franny's habitual cursing, and even John's, although not encouraged, are not actively curbed,
despite Mother's occasional disapproval. Instead, the
children are free to roam around the hotel exercising
their imaginations and developing their interests.
Franny and John enjoy listening in on guests on the
hotel's intercom system, especially when they over-

hear lovemaking noises. In the hotel John is introduced to sex by Ronda Ray, a worker who keeps a
room there, and there, too, he develops a close
relationship with his grandfather, Coach Bob, who
teaches him weight-lifting and body building. Coach
Bob's room, where he works out, becomes like the
wrestling room in *Garp*, a sanctuary and a place of
peace, like a womb within a womb.

But whereas the hotel is an image of peace,
Irving suggests that life itself is not wholly peaceful,
for Frank has brought Sorrow into the hotel. It is
because of Sorrow that Coach Bob dies: while he and
John are working out in his room, the stuffed dog
suddenly falls out of the closet and shocks Coach Bob
into a fatal heart attack. Then, during a New Year's
Eve party a few days later, John succeeds in luring
Bitty Tuck to a room, hoping finally to have sex with
someone his own age. In the bathroom, while insert-
ing her diaphragm, she finds Sorrow in the bathtub,
and screams and faints. Thanatos, as Sigmund Freud
wrote, exists in the energy of Eros.

Death's human specter reappears shortly after
that incident. The party ended and the guests gone
home, John sees in the darkness a man dressed in a
white dinner jacket, passed out in the snow. He brings
the man into the hotel, revives him, and then tries to
make him leave. Escorting the man out the front
door, John notices the mail, including a letter from
Freud, inviting the family to help him run his hotel in
Vienna. Once again Freud's influence and the vision
of a man in a white dinner jacket coincide to change
Father's life. Glimpsing the man as he fades into the
snowy night, Father calls after him, hoping this time
to understand the secret, the message: " 'Good-bye!
Good luck! Good-bye!' called the voice of the man in
the white dinner jacket, and my father stood staring

into the darkness until the wind chilled him and he shivered in his bathrobe and slippers; he let me pull him inside."

Father remains, once again, in the dark, but the specter's appearance is to have dire consequences for the family. Accepting Freud's invitation to come to Vienna, Father sells the hotel to a circus of midgets called Fritz's Act, and the family prepares to leave, traveling on separate planes. The plane carrying Mother and Egg, and the stuffed dog he has become attached to, crashes, and the rescuers are able to find the bodies when they spot the stuffed Sorrow bobbing up and down in the ocean. Irving writes, "Sorrow floats"—which becomes the code phrase for the anxiety that dominates the novel.

In accordance with the first stage of Campbell's monomyth—"separation"—the children are removed from the comforting world of the first hotel and asked to travel to a strange land. The violence of this removal is underscored by the death of Mother, the children's only real parent, and the stabilizing influence in the home. As the children enter the second stage of their adventure, *three* of the family members are gone: Coach Bob, Mother, and Egg; five are left to face a very different world. Franny immediately recognizes the need to understand the Under Toad/ Sorrow: "It was Franny who said, later, that we must all watch out for what form Sorrow would take *next;* we must learn to recognize the different poses." Lilly, who will never be able to get beyond her childhood (it has been diagnosed that she has stopped growing and will be a dwarf, and her emotional growth is stunted as well) thinks that ". . . Fritz's Act would have been smaller and easier to live with—all around." John expresses their common separation anxiety most straightforwardly: "we had arrived in a foreign country."

Their stay in Vienna corresponds to the children's "initiation"—the second stage of the mythic adventure—wherein they descend into a strange world and there learn lessons that will help them upon their return. The historical anecdotage of *fin de siècle* Vienna, which the children study before their trip, colors their outlook on their new home and accords somewhat with what they learn there. These historical details, however, emphasize Irving's thematic concern more than they reveal the Vienna of 1957–1964, which the children actually experience. For the Vienna of this novel is almost as insular as the American setting, being as totally dominated by the milieu of the second Hotel New Hampshire as Dairy, New Hampshire, had been overshadowed by the first hotel. The museumlike city, which so profoundly affected Garp and Irving's previous protagonists, does not intrude here upon the hermetic world of the family fairy tale.

The Vienna of the late nineteenth century, which does appeal to the children's imagination, was a city in the midst of social disintegration. Austrian liberalism, which had taken control of the government in midcentury, was falling out of favor with the people. New social groups clamored for political participation, including anti-Semitic Christian Socialists. In 1895, Emperor Francis Joseph I, with the support of the Catholic hierarchy, refused to sanction the election of Karl Lueger, an anti-Semite, as mayor of Vienna. By 1900, however, the liberal power was broken. Carl Schorske writes that the liberals "had been crushed by modern mass movements, Christian, anti-Semitic, socialist, and nationalist."[19] The defeat of the liberals produced profound psychological despair—Schorske describes the mood as "one not so much of decadence as of impotence," and then explains: "Anxiety, impotence, a heightened awareness of the brutality of social existence: these features assumed new centrality in a social climate where the creed of liberalism was being shattered by events."[20] Despite its turmoil, Viennese society strove to maintain an outward glitter and elegance, the people all but worshiping their crown prince, Rudolf. Ironically, despite his stately air, Rudolf himself was truly emblematic of his city in his tortured psychic state and lurking sense of despair. Anonymously he wrote polemics for a liberal newspaper and he would shock his country and the world by shooting himself and a mistress at his retreat, Mayerling, in the Vienna Woods in 1889.

The historical details Irving mentions briefly concern the prince, but mostly he concentrates on the artists who were coming of age in Vienna at that time: Arthur Schnitzler, Gustav Klimt, Gustav Mahler, Anton Bruckner, and Sigmund Freud. In particular, Irving emphasizes some decadent details— Schnitzler's record lovemaking 464 times within one year with his "sweet girl" Jeanette Heger, Prince Rudolf's relationship with Mitzi Caspar, and Bruckner's fondling the skulls of Schubert and Beethoven when their graves were opened for scientific study— most of them supporting Freud's dictum that Vienna was an elaborate facade for concealing sexual reality.

Many of the Viennese artists lived consistently with the kind of art they were producing, an ultra-aesthetic art, making of their art a refuge, an escape from the political realities of the time—in Schorske's words, "The life of art became a substitute for the life of action."[21] From this troubled climate emerged the art that has had profound effects on all twentieth-

century art and thought—its primary influence involving the discovery of psychological man, no longer
merely a rational creature, but a feeling and instinctual one as well. The innovations in art and thought
introduced by Freud, Schnitzler, and Klimt were
ignored by their peers, denounced, inevitably, as
innovation destructive to established values. Frederic
Morton, however, defends the art of these rebels:

> These "destroyers" only rendered audible or visible or
> thinkable a distress already existing and deepening
> with the forward march of occidental culture. Their
> innovations were really alarms of loss, or dreams of
> restoration. The angst in Mahler's huge surges
> clutched at primal beginnings. Freud reached for
> pre-Puritan libido. Herzl called for a return to the land
> of milk and honey. Klimt contorted his nudes into
> ancient Oriental opulence. Bruckner cried out for the
> freshness that lay forgotten in folk and faith.[22]

Morton goes on to quote from the *Tagblatt*, one of
Vienna's leading papers, on the emptiness of the
threatened status quo: "Outside, everything is gleam
and gorgeousness. One lives only on the outside, one
is led astray by the dancing phosphorescence . . . one
no longer expects anything from the inner life, from
thinking or believing."[23] Irving obviously sees a parallel between the spiritual disintegration of the *fin de
siècle* and his own era, particularly in the abandon-
ment of the inner life in favor of a "dancing phosphorescence." His prescription is a return to the
Brucknerian freshness of the fairy tale, a return to
primal beginnings, to the world of magic and dreams.
In this way he is akin to the artists he mentions in his
novel, hoping to address our hearts and souls as they
did.

One of the children's favorite anecdotes from

that time is the story of the King of the Mice, recounted to them by Freud:

> THERE WAS A STREET CLOWN CALLED KING OF THE MICE: HE TRAINED RODENTS, HE DID HOROSCOPES, HE COULD IMPERSONATE NAPOLEON, HE COULD MAKE DOGS FART ON COMMAND. ONE NIGHT HE JUMPED OUT HIS WINDOW WITH ALL HIS PETS IN A BOX. WRITTEN ON THE BOX WAS THIS: "LIFE IS SERIOUS BUT ART IS FUN!"

This story is based on that of Johann Pfeiffer, "King of the Birds," a Viennese sidewalk entertainer who killed himself by jumping out of an open window in 1889. His slogan, "Life is serious but art is fun," corresponds to Irving's own aesthetic credo: in the face of life, art should be fun, magical, and restorative. It is Johann's fate that gives birth to the recurring phrase, "Keep passing the open windows," encapsulating the children's recognition that the basic principle of living well and wisely is simple survival. This, too, is the function of art, certainly that of fairy tales, to convince the reader of the essential value of life itself as potential success and happiness. Irving feels that much modern art has lost sight of this function, and in this novel/tale he strives to remind us by invoking both art's primal sources and its modern heritage.

When the family joins Freud at the Gasthaus Freud, later to become the second Hotel New Hampshire, they find that Freud's hair has turned white and he is blind. Later it is revealed that he went blind in a concentration camp: "They had performed some failed experiment with his eyes. . . ." Freud is properly proud that he survived this horror, that he outsmarted Herr Tod (Mr. Death)—he has experienced the Under Toad/Sorrow in its most grotesque form, in the violent climax of what began in *fin de siècle* Vienna (Hitler was born in 1889, the year of Mayerling.). Whatever "the other Freud" might have made of Auschwitz, Buchenwald, and Babi Yar—they certainly cannot be accounted for in any conventional understanding of the "pleasure principle"—the Holocaust must compel acknowledgment of the existence of a deathly force of monstrous capacity. Irving's Freud's ability to go beyond this supreme manifestation of Thanatos is, again, a celebration of the life force over death. His survival is an example from which the Berry family must learn in this city of death, as they struggle to confront and deal with their own losses.

The family also meets Freud's new bear, "a smart bear," named Susie. It soon becomes apparent that Susie is not a real bear, but a woman in a bear suit. Susie masquerades as a bear because she is ashamed of her own ugliness: "I am the original not-bad-if-you-put-a-bag-over-her-head girl." She, too, has been raped, and when she learns of Franny's rape and her attempt to deal with it by not dealing with it, Susie is outraged, lecturing Franny about the need to be angry about her experience and to deal with it actively. Susie and Franny grow to be close friends— Susie will eventually help Franny come to grips with the rape, and Franny will help Susie gain confidence in herself, encouraging her sense of self-worth by engaging in a temporary homosexual relationship with her. When Frank and John come upon them in bed one day, the boys are horrified, likening Susie in her bear suit to Sorrow, but this is an immature reaction, for the relationship ultimately proves helpful for both young women.

The second Hotel New Hampshire, like the first, is not a real hotel; few actual guests ever stay there. Instead, it houses two groups of permanent tenants: some prostitutes, who use the hotel at night, and a coterie of radicals, who occupy the hotel's top floor during the day. Along with Susie and Freud, the prostitutes and the radicals dominate the children's landscape in Vienna, their interactions with these two groups overshadowing any experience of the city beyond this hotel society. Neither the radicals nor the prostitutes develop three-dimensional personalities; all are grotesque caricatures, each known principally by a particular personality trait or quirk, as is indicated, again, by their names: Screaming Annie, Arbeiter, Wrench, and the like. The senior members of each respective group even share the same name, Old Billig—thus Irving makes clear that there is little difference between them:

> They both believed in the commercial possibilites of a simple ideal: they both believed they could, one day, be "free." They both thought that their own bodies were objects easily sacrificed for a cause (and easily restored, or replaced, after the hardship of the sacrifice). Even their names were similar—if for different reasons.

The simplicity of their ideals and the illusion of possible "freedom" readily mark these two bands of freaks as aberrant specimens in Irving's world, false models of the id and ego, irresponsibile purveyors of the commodities of sex and violence. The children must learn, somehow, to deal with the perversions they represent, to resist their false examples and to go on to truer images of Eros and Thanatos—the revolutionaries, of course, are to prove the more dangerous adversary.

The children react to their new environment in different ways. The narrator feels that he cannot grow: "I knew I would never really grow up; I knew my childhood would never leave me, and I would never be quite adult enough—quite responsible enough—for the world." Meanwhile, he remains obsessed with lifting weights and with his love for his sister. He also visits some of the prostitutes in the hotel; his sexual experiences are still strictly physical, and John unconsciously realizes that he will need a more fulfilling sexual relationship before he can grow. He tries to develop such a relationship with Fehlgeburt, one of the radical women, and on the night that she confides to him the radicals' plan to blow up the Vienna Opera, they make love. However, Fehlgeburt treats this act objectively as a necessary life experience, something she must do at least once before martyring herself in the car that is to destroy the Opera—again, love dances with death. For John the evening is empty and depressing; he describes the experience as "desperate and joyless as any sex in the second Hotel New Hampshire ever was." When, later that night, the troubled Fehlgeburt commits suicide, the sex in the hotel and the radicals are thematically implicated with death. Both are antilife, and anti-love.

Although John fears that he cannot grow, the novel demonstrates that he will. His sister Lilly, on the other hand, is truly unable to grow up. She cannot cope with the politics and sex of the second hotel, nor with the lessons of history to which she is exposed in Vienna. Lilly accompanies the other children when Freud takes them on tours of the city; she sees the plaque memorializing those murdered by the Gestapo and learns about the concentration camps. It is a lesson reinforced by visits to the Judenplatz, the old Jewish quarter of the city:

Freud would call out to apartments that were no longer apartments. He would identify whole buildings that were no longer there. And the *people* he used to know there—they weren't there, either. It was a tour of things we couldn't see, but Freud saw them still; he saw 1939, and before, when he'd last been in the Juden-platz with a working pair of eyes.

They see things that enforce not only Vienna's sexual license (prostitution is legal), but also its hypocrisy, and Freud also takes them to the Imperial Vault, where the Hapsburgs are buried, without their hearts, which were interred elsewhere—Freud explains, "history separates everthing."

Lilly also becomes very close to Fehlgeburt, and is deeply affected by the selections which Fehlgeburt (an American literature major at the university) reads to them. Lilly attempts to retreat into literature, to "grow" by becoming a writer. Her book is the story of her own family, with everyone in a heroic role; she titles it "Trying to Grow." But Lilly is unable to get beyond the death of her mother, and the lessons about death she has learned in Vienna. Her book ends with the plane crash, for she is unable to go imaginatively beyond that. Like the terminally embryonic Egg, who could not survive the separation from the womblike first hotel, Lilly is a true example of stunted growth, her physical dwarfism serving to indicate the inadequacy of her personality to meet the emotional demands of adulthood. She will live on into the return stage of the Berry family fairy-tale adventure, but she has clearly failed to keep up with her siblings' maturation, and to assimilate the complex experience of Vienna, and so she will not be able to share in the rewards of happy adjustment later. Frank aptly describes Lilly's world view as "real *Weltschmerz* (world hurt)."

Frank seems to thrive in Vienna, growing closer to his siblings, especially to John and Franny, and gradually assuming the leadership role that was Franny's in the first Hotel New Hampshire. Being the most conversant in German, he adapts best to the new environment and helps acclimate his family to their strange surroundings. He never seemed uncomfortable with his homosexuality, even as a young teenager, but the Viennese milieu apparently helps to confirm his acceptance of it. He seems to identify with Prince Rudolf, who grew desperate and resorted finally to suicide because of the conflicts arising from a life of poses and hypocrisy. Frank manages to accept himself, and in the process rejects beliefs of all kinds:

> A near-violent atheist, Frank would turn to believing only in Fate—in random fortune or random doom, in arbitrary slapstick and arbitrary sorrow. He would become a preacher *against* every bill of goods anyone ever was sold. . . .
> Frank believed in *zap!* He believed in surprises. He was in constant attack and retreat, and he was equally, constantly, wide-eyed and goofily stumbling about in the sudden sunlight—tripping across the wasteland littered with bodies from the darkness of just a moment ago.

Although thus embattled by a world he views as chaotic and violent, Frank has succeeded in developing a stable personality, confident of himself and poised against all possible adversity.

Franny, on the other hand, is apparently driven to continued involvement with the forces of violence and promiscuous sexuality. She becomes a kind of dual personality, loving and protective within the family, haunted by the lure of evil without. She

decides to mother her brothers and sister, primarily
by deflating the poses they adopt to avoid the world:
Frank's nihilism, Lilly's determination to grow by
writing, Susie's bearishness, John's infatuation with
herself. Franny announces that since Mother and
Iowa Bob, "the shit detectors," are gone, "I'm left to
detect it. I point out the shit—that's my role." This is
easy enough for Franny, who seems naturally interested in "shit." Unfortunately, she becomes infatuat-
ed with Ernst, the most sinister of the revolutionaries
and also a writer of, and lecturer on, pornography.
When the other children read his pornography, it
gives them "headaches and dry throats," but it has no
such effect on Franny, and she continues to seek out
Ernst and to listen to his descriptions of exotic sexual
positions. John finds Ernst reminiscent of Chipper
Dove—they are linked by their delicate hands—and
he gets to the heart of Franny's attraction to Ernst
when he writes:

> And I knew then, too, what it was that Franny saw in
> Ernst. It was more than a physical resemblance to
> Chipper Dove, it was that cocksure quality, that touch
> of evil, that hint of destruction, that icy leadership—
> that was what could sneak its way into my sister's heart,
> that was what captured the *her in her,* that was what
> took Franny's strength away.

Franny eventually has sex with Ernst to experience
his perverse fascination firsthand.

Franny's vulnerability begins to surface during
this stage of the tale. Despite her claims of self-
confidence and her insistence on the need to be
herself, she is still troubled by her rape and by the
death of her mother. She becomes especially depen-
dent upon Susie for her love and advice, finding in

the bear-woman a combined mother substitute and lover whose symbolic, psychological appropriateness adds another fairy-tale touch to this case of adolescent trauma. John sees that Susie is a good influence on Franny, and Franny admits to him that she feels safe with Susie, that ". . . it's easier to love someone of your own sex. There's not quite so much to commit yourself to, there's not so much to risk."

It is in Vienna that Franny and John acknowledge the depth of their love for each other. After his depressing sexual encounter with Fehlgeburt, John ponders the illusion of politics and revolutionary action, the illusion of "waiting for things to become something else." Overwhelmed by his own stifling emotions, he decides to seek out a prostitute for comfort, but, instead, finds himself running into his sister's arms. They kiss passionately and decide that they will one day have to sleep together, though Franny cautions that they must wait until they will be able to handle it, when it will be safer.

The stay in the second Hotel New Hampshire comes to a true fairy-tale ending, as the revolutionaries put their plan of blowing up the Opera into effect. On the previous day, Father and John passed a man in a white dinner jacket on the street, but Father (becoming ever blinder to such omens) did not notice. The revolutionaries hold the Berry family hostage and insist that Freud drive the car with the bomb. When Ernst brags about his sexual involvement with Franny, Father kills him with the baseball bat Freud uses in place of a cane. This confuses the revolutionaries, who are lost without their leader, but they insist on going ahead with their plan. Freud then assumes the hero's mantle, striking the car-bomb with his bat, blowing himself up with the car and foiling the revolutionaries' plan. During the explosion Father is blinded, becoming literally what he has long been, blind to all external reality.

In Vienna the children have been marooned in a landscape of sad history, violent politics, and serious sexuality—it is a vision of a world of chaos where no one is safe. In the lobby of the second Hotel New Hampshire, where the final violence takes place, Franny and John recognize the lessons of Sorrow:

> In the bad light in the lobby of the second Hotel New Hampshire, Franny and I could be fooled into thinking we saw shapes of Sorrow when we saw nothing at all. But hadn't Sorrow taught us to be on guard, to look *everywhere*? Sorrow can take any shape in the world.

Appreciating the need to "keep passing the open windows," they face the challenge of choosing how to live now that they fully understand how illusory was Father's dream of a life lived in hotels.

The novel's final two chapters constitute what Campbell labels "the return":

> The full round, the norm of the monomyth, requires that the hero shall now begin the labor of bringing the runes of wisdom, the Golden Fleece, or his sleeping princess, back into the kingdom of humanity, where the boon may redound to the renewing of the community, the nation, the planet, or the ten thousand worlds.[24]

Unfortunately, at this point in the story, Irving suddenly seems to lose control of his material—some of the scenes that follow seem overdone, others poorly handled or simply extraneous. The family returns to the United States newly wealthy from the sale of

Lilly's book, which has been helped by the notoriety the family received in thwarting the plan of the revolutionaries. They first stop in New York City, where they stay at the Stanhope Hotel. Lilly falls in love with this hotel and decides to live there; Franny is to stay with her for a while. Frank, who becomes a successful agent (having represented Lilly), gets an apartment nearby, and Father and John move in with him.

Shortly after their arrival, John and Franny go through with their uncontrollable desire to make love to each other. Irving's stylistic trademark has always been the use of fantastic exaggeration to penetrate and reveal psychological truth; this is also the method of fairy tales, as Bettelheim has argued: the externalizing of internal processes. Neither Irving nor his narrator is actually advocating incest, but, as Franny has taken over her mother's function, the scene can be read as the fulfillment of John's Oedipal dream. And this dream enactment has positive consequences for both of them, because Franny realizes that she must overdo the lovemaking so that John will come to understand how destructive their relationship must become if it continues, miring them both in the romance of childhood. Therefore, they make love so many times that the experience becomes a painful one: "In a way—if I had *stayed* in love with her—she would have been the death of me; we would have been the death of each other. But she simply overdid it; she knew exactly what she was doing."

Thus brother and sister are released from their stifling mutual attachment and are ready to lead emotionally independent lives. Thus, the incident corresponds to various fairy-tale patterns involving familial relationships: self-realization is a painful experience. In the fairy tale "Brother and Sister," Bettelheim points out, ". . . the brother represents an endangered aspect of an essentially inseparable unity, and the sister, as symbol of motherly care once one has become alienated from home, is the rescuer."[25] Franny, too, rescues John and helps him to achieve integration—as he writes at the end of that experience, "everything is a fairy tale."

On the way home from this meeting, John meets Chipper Dove on the street. In the manner of the fairy tale, Irving here is bringing his "villain" back for the necessary punishment—all evildoers must get their just rewards if the tale is to perform its reassuring function. The handling of the revenge sequence, however, undercuts the point. Meeting him in the middle of the street, John lifts Chipper Dove in his arms, squeezes him, and then puts him down—it is an elegant symbolic image of nonviolent revenge, for what John has done is to capture Chipper in a "bear hug." During the confrontation with the revolutionaries in Vienna, John actually killed one of them in this way; here he manages to restrain himself, limiting his assault to an intimidating demonstration of his new physical power. Having grown and doggedly developed his body's strength—which is, like all strength in Irving's world, strikingly bear-like—John shows here that he can control his aggressive, id-directed response to a given situation (this adversary poses no direct threat), and thus that he is now truly ready to become the hero of the story.

Unfortunately, Irving, apparently not content with this eloquent gesture, proceeds to elaborate the family's revenge, rendering literal the retaliatory bear hug and so undercutting the supposed new maturity of his protagonists. Presumably motivated by the serious intention of releasing Franny from the fear of men that is now revealed as the legacy of her unresolved rape trauma, the children devise a plot to humiliate their old enemy. Following a play script contributed by Lilly, they lure Chipper Dove to Franny's room, where Susie, in her bear costume, threatens to rape him. This retributive rape is not consummated, but Chipper is effectively reduced to a frightened, snivelling wretch who runs from the room with his pants down. The problem here is that so much effort and so much tension is being invested, at a clearly climactic moment in the novel, in what is essentially only another childish prank. Treating of a grimly serious subject, the crime of rape—with which Irving has elsewhere (in *Garp*, as well as in other sections of this novel) shown himself responsibly concerned—the author and his protagonists settle for a simplistic and shallow reciprocal threat, ganging up gleefully to reduce the villain of eight years past to a moment of panic. Somehow the poetic justice of their revenge seems inadequate to the realistic tragedy of Franny's rape trauma, as if Irving is struggling for catharsis of a real-life hurt by means of make-believe therapy; the fairy tale's rigorous standard of proportional consequences is lost. In the process, moreover, Irving manages to make unsympathetic figures of his protagonists, especially Frank, who, inexplicably, jumps up and down on a bed in a leotard, taunting the victim with his own homosexuality. The others act more like the Viennese revolutionaries, obsessed with their futile gesture of protest, than like successfully grown personalities who can deal maturely with their sense of outrage.

Shortly after this, Lilly commits suicide, frustrated by her inability to live up to the challenge of being an important writer, which for her represents adult status. She remains firmly rooted in childhood, unable to make the imaginative leap that is necessary for her to write a really important work, and so, like the King of Mice, she jumps out a window to her death. Her death is structurally appropriate in the novel's scheme, because of Lilly's physical and emotional inability to grow up. Again, unfortunately, Irving does not stop here, but appends an extended, wholly unnecessary section on the cult of suicide in universities and on the tendency to equate suicide by literary figures with artistic seriousness. Then, losing his thread entirely, Irving goes on to attack the tendency in academic circles to mistake muddled, incoherent writing for art. Whatever its merits, the diatribe seems wholly out of place in a fairy tale, symptomatic perhaps of some personal grudge unrelated to this novel. This is also true of Irving's repeated reference to the poetry of Donald Justice, whose considerations of suicide and aging are quoted throughout the last two chapters. Again, regardless of the poems' merit, they are awkwardly introduced, remain only vaguely related to the novel's themes, and simply distract from them.

Irving's concluding pages, however, work beautifully. Father decides that he would like to buy the Arbuthnot-by-the-Sea, and Frank and John go to California to buy it from the owner (old Arbuthnot, the man in the white dinner jacket) who is dying—a hopeful omen, surely, for the Berry family, whose security will be ensured by the passing of their nemesis, the specter of death. The hotel, which had remained a ruin, is restored, and Father and John move in. John now becomes the caretaker of his father's persistent illusions, while Frank pursues a successful career in New York, and Franny, who has become a famous actress, lives in California, where she is married to Junior Jones.

Although the third Hotel New Hampshire is certainly the nicest hotel the family ever owned, it is even less hotel than the others, for it houses only Father and John. John caters to his father's illusion that there are guests, but the hotel never really serves that purpose. Instead, it serves as another retreat from the world—finally, the safe place that Father always envisioned. Thus the story returns to where it began, in the magical world of Father's memory. Now physically imprisoned (by his blindness) in his illusory world, Father remains the perfect embodiment of Sigmund Freud's definition of the dreamer (Father has Freud's works read to him after his blindness). In *The Interpretation of Dreams*, Freud speaks of the dreamer as one who ignores the restraints of daytime thinking; thus the dream gives him what reality denies—the fulfillment of his secret wishes. Dreams comfort, strengthen, and ward off emptiness: "Dreams are disconnected, they accept the most violent contradictions without the least objection, they admit impossibilities, they disregard knowledge which carries great weight in the daytime."[26] (In all this they are akin to fairy tales, as Freud himself recognized.) Father's blindness keeps the daytime out, ensuring that he will remain forever in the world of night, the world of dreams.

For John, too, the hotel is a strategic retreat, for here his own metamorphosis is finally completed. One night he is awakened by a bear, which crawls into his bed—it is Susie, and John is overjoyed because he realizes that he has been in love with her for some time. The scene is a reversal of the Beauty and the Beast tale, which Bettelheim classifies as an "animal groom" story, for here the woman is disguised as an animal and released from her spell by the love of a man. The basic thematic structures, however, remain intact: Susie is a beast to herself because she feels that she is ugly and because she, like Franny, still suffers the trauma of her rape, whereas John has not managed to recognize his love for her before this because of his own emotional immaturity (his previous sexual experiences have all been purely physical or psychological ones). Their love represents, in Bettelheim's words, "the healing of the pernicious break between the animal and the higher aspects of man. . . . the end point of an evolution from self-centered, immature sexuality to one that finds its fulfillment in a human relation of deep devotion."[27] In the marriage of Beauty and the Beast is portrayed the "humanization and socialization of the id by the superego,"[28] and this is what happens in the third hotel, which is itself a kind of superego, a sheltering place where one's fullest personality development may be realized.

John and Susie marry, and the hotel becomes a rape crisis center, a healing place for the spiritually maimed. Father's ideal conception of a hotel thus becomes reality:

> ". . . that's just what a good hotel does: it simply provides you with the space, and with the atmosphere, for what it is you *need*. A good hotel turns space and atmosphere into something generous, into something sympathetic—a good hotel makes those gestures that are like touching you, or saying a kind word to you, just when (and *only* when) you need it. A good hotel is always there. . . ."

This is also the boon that John, the hero, wants to pass on in his narrative, for this is also the function of the fairy tale and the novel. The power of love, in its various incarnations, at appropriate stages of life, is recognized as the transforming device. Although Irving insists here, as elsewhere, that sex without love and devotion is animallike, he recognizes also that the animal aspects of human nature can be charming and nonthreatening (as in fairy tales). As Susie's story proves, one's animal nature must be befriended and respected if its beastly, destructive instincts are to be controlled and subdued to the development of the total personality. In keeping with the "Beauty and the Beast" motif, it is Father who encourages John to marry Susie—although this father never manages to integrate himself fully into life, at least his son may do so.

The transcendent nature of the ending is enforced when Franny calls John and Susie to announce that she is pregnant and that she wants them to take her child. Franny and Junior Jones recognize that John and Susie will be perfect parents and the third hotel will provide the perfect environment—for Father's expression of the ideal of a good hotel is an eloquent and touching definition, expressed by a very imperfect parent, of the ideal of parenthood itself. Inhabiting this preeminently human and sheltering environment—in which both the blind idealism of the male dreamer and the spiritual pain of the female sufferer are provided for—John and Susie have made of this hotel the home that the others failed to be, and so Franny's child, a product of a love beyond sexuality, is to be the heir to the lessons of the tale, the child of the future. In fairy tales it is not important where the child comes from; its appearance is always miraculous. And in John Irving's universe, parenthood is the highest state one can achieve—it is the apotheosis of development. For this reason, John is the hero of this novel, for he alone among the Berry children will achieve parenthood; he will be the ideal father.

The novel concludes on a snowy night when a family from Arizona, having lost its way, is invited to stay at the Hotel New Hampshire—its first guests. The following morning, John convinces Susie to put on her bear suit once more, so that the children can see a bear before they leave. She does so, to the children's delight: they have been given a glimpse of a magical, primal world, a gift to take with them through life: "The bear that paused by the woodpile, its breath a fog upon the bright, cold morning, its paws softly denting the fresh, untouched snow—as if it were the first bear on earth, as if this was the planet's first snow—*all* of it had been convincing."

At the end, John and Susie are awaiting the birth of Franny's baby, which is how a fairy tale is supposed to end, as Bettelheim points out: "While fairy tales invariably point the way to a better future, they concentrate on the process of change, rather than describing the exact details of the bliss eventually to be gained."[29] There is no need for completed histories, as in *Garp*; Irving has brought us as far as we need to go.

While at the first Hotel New Hampshire, Iowa Bob one day passes on his philosophy to the family. It is his theory that,

> We were all on a big ship—on a big cruise around the world. And in spite of the danger of being swept away, at any time, or perhaps because of the danger, we were not *allowed* to be depressed or unhappy. The way the world worked *was* not cause for some sort of blanket cynicism or sophomoric despair. . . . The way the world worked—which was badly—was just a strong

incentive to live purposefully, and to be determined about living well.

Iowa Bob is this novel's Marcus Aurelius. This is the lesson of the fairy tale, which also teaches that one must rule oneself wisely and as a consequence, live happily. And this is what John's tale demonstrates, although, like the hero that he is, he leaves us with a vision of transcendence.

# CHAPTER 7

# An Interview with John Irving (Bread Loaf, Vermont; August 17, 1981)

GM: It seems that all the protagonists in your novels have fathers who are dead, absent, or indifferent: Siggy's father and Garp's father are dead, Trumper's father and the father of the narrator of *The 158-Pound Marriage* are distant or cold; even the father in *The Hotel New Hampshire,* though the most vital of them, is ineffective. The mother is usually a more dominant, commanding figure. If you wanted to psychoanalyze yourself, what would you make of this recurring pattern in your novels?

JI: Well, I think less for any reasons that are personal, but mainly just from observations of families that I've known, it is my experience of contemporary America that the mother seems to establish the tone for the children; the father is not so much an absent figure, or a cool or aloof figure, but you have to see him as he compares to the mother, and in almost every case of the people I've been close to, I would say that something of the mother's character is more pervasive than the father's in most families. I don't know that I'm an absent father myself, but I'm probably not as present as my wife is.

GM: But the children of these fathers always seem to become very attentive fathers themselves:

Trumper is a very attentive father, Garp is an attentive father, etc. . . .

JI: I suppose I feel fortunate as a writer that I can be a much more present parent than someone who goes out to an early morning job and comes home just before dark—even if I'm distracted much of the time, or living in a world of my own most of the time, or even if the kids are aware of it, or they suddenly discover I'm working when, wandering around the house, I say, "Cut that out, I'm trying to work," and I may impose on them that way. I suppose I'm aware that I have an advantage over my father, who worked in school and taught and still does, and is someone whom I always saw leaving the house in the morning and coming back at night, and though he was very present during vacations and in the evening —in fact, my own father did a lot of shopping and the cooking—if you called the house in the middle of the day, you didn't get him, and if you were sick, he didn't bring you the hot chocolate or whatever. I've taken some pleasure in being sort of a homebody. It's one of the things that appeals to me, or that did appeal to me when I was teaching, that I simply didn't have to be as absent as a lot of parents have to be, and I like that. When I had, suddenly, the means to get myself a studio, an office, or someplace to go to and shut myself in, I simply did not want to avail myself of that. Maybe it's a coincidence . . . I suppose it does reflect, though, that I feel happy to have the opportunity to be more at home than I would if I were doing something else.

GM: But if the father is at home as much as the mother, then he can be as much of an influence—or do you still think the mother would still be the dominating influence on the children's lives?

JI: Well, it depends on the age, doesn't it, and it also depends on the sex of the child. When the children are small, it seems to me that the mother is the really reliable source, because usually in working situations, if something goes wrong, and somebody has to take up the slack, it's usually the mother who has to do it. At the same time, though, as your kids get older—my kids were both boys—I find that I have much more of a relationship with them than I did when they were small—more of a relationship with them than my wife has with them. If they were girls, I guess, there would be more of a sense of drawing them closer to her. I really haven't drawn any conclusions outside the fiction. Of course, the father, now, in *The Hotel New Hampshire* is a figure who lives largely in his imagination, but he's so much more of a character than the mother in a number of ways that I think I've changed that somewhat in this book, and in the book I'm thinking of next there is quite exclusively a father-son relationship; I don't even know if I'm going to introduce the mother as a character. At the point at which the book begins, she's gone—it's just the father and the son—I don't think I'll even do much with her in the flashbacks.

There may be a more technical reason for doing this, which is why so many writers are attracted to making their characters orphans—not just a writer like Dickens, who was interested in orphans for other reasons—but the orphan in literature is appealing for the simple reason that the author is then free to invent the background. You're not responsible for these lineages that have to be taken seriously, and it is simply a matter of focus. In a novel like *Garp*, for example, I knew I had a lot of characters and a lot of territory to cover, and there was no way I could have a father and a mother and not dissipate my attention. Since he was going to have one or the other, and the whole nursing notion was present in my mind, I felt that I had to get rid of the father as quickly as

possible. In that way, I think, the novelist may tend to
be interested in single parents—not in the contemporary sense of "single parent"—because it's a conve-
nience. Look at *Great Expectations,* for example—it
begins in the graveyard where he looks at all the
members of the family he doesn't have to write
about—they don't have to be characters—it just lets Jo
bring him up, and it's convenient—it's like saying all
these characters aren't going to be really important.

GM: Another motif is the maturing or formative
experience of the American protagonists in your
novels, which generally comes as a result of an
extended stay in Europe, in Vienna. Are you reworking that Jamesian theme of the traditions of Europe
versus the naiveté of America—do you feel that one
cannot mature successfully in America, or do you
feel, specifically as a writer of the 60s, 70s, and 80s,
that in this particular time in America one cannot
come to an understanding of the world—to use a
term you like to use—growing up in America?

JI: I don't want to make that sound like an
intellectual premise, which, for James of course, it
certainly was. In my own case, I think Europe was a
necessary journey for me, not so much for cultural
sophistication or for maturing in any kind of intellectual way, as for accomplishing what Auden used to
call "the act of noticing," when he said all writing that
was any good really came from the heightened ability
to *notice,* and of course, he meant to notice imaginatively, too—not simply to remember, but to see things
freshly. I'm sure my European experience was like
the experience of many American writers—I didn't
really ever feel myself an exile, or ever really feel like
an expatriate, although once, for a long period of
time, I did feel like I'd never come back to America.
But, more importantly, to me, or I think, to any
writer, it's absolutely vital to go to some place that's

foreign to you. I would think it would be just as
important for a Frenchman to go to England, or a
Frenchman to come to America, or an Englishman to
come here . . . I don't think this is a particularly
American inadequacy. In the nineteenth century, it
may have been, but I, for one, am not intimidated by
European culture, and in terms of its contemporary
output, I'm hardly intimidated by its literature. I
think the best literature being written in the world
right now is being written in this country—certainly
the best literature in English. Britain really should
stop pulling rank on us—they haven't had writers to
match ours for some time. Simply because they used
our language first, they still have that tendency to
presume that they use it better, and they don't. The
language—the *language* is not being used best by the
English today; it's being used best by the Americans.
And when I speak of today, I mean for some time.

What was impressive to me the first time I went
to Europe was how being in a foreign country with
another language forced you to notice all commonplace things. For sure, there's an introduction to a
culture that was foreign to me, but more impressive
to me in a way, and more important to my development as a writer, was that it caused me to notice
mayonnaise and mustard and what the sugar came in,
because I had to learn another word for it, because I
had to get used to the fact that the mayonnaise was in
a *tube* instead of a jar, that the way the butter pat was
cut was flatter and more rectangular. It didn't make
me fall in love with Europe and find all those things
so special—instead, it made me remember what butter was like when I was fifteen on the coast of Maine.
This is frequently the American experience: Hemingway went to Paris to write well about Michigan; he'd
come back to Ketchum, Idaho, and he'd write well
about Europe. We're always behind ourselves: Joyce

went to Trieste and to Paris and wrote about Dublin. You need to *get away*, to go outside of yourself to see clearly not so much where you are as where you've *been*. And there's nothing like that exposure to something novel. I'm not speaking personally—I mean as a writer, that is the advantage and the value to me of places far away.

GM: In connection with that—this is not assuming that you are a social realist, which you're not . . .

JI: Thank you.

GM: . . . but there is a preoccupation . . . when you write about Europe, you're very conscious of historical details. European history comes alive, but you never allude to any American historical event—except that I think I remember you have twice mentioned the assassination of Kennedy. . . .

JI: Which I regret mentioning, by the way, in *both* cases. No, you're quite right—that's very clear. But you see, here's what happened: I don't want to say that Vienna for me could have been Cleveland, or in the case of Garp, that he could have gone with his mother to Cleveland—though in the film, he'll go with her to New York; maybe that's foreign enough. What I'm saying is, you have to go away from home, wherever home is, and it's *home* that causes you to notice things. I mean, people died—you don't have to go to Vienna to die; you don't have to go to the Pension Grillparzer to be decadent; you don't, in the case of *The Hotel New Hampshire,* have to go to Vienna to discover either prostitution or terrorism, *but* you will notice them more when everything is foreign to you. And, of course, in the case of *The Hotel New Hampshire,* the foreign country those children *really* go to is the place we all go when we're forced to grow up too soon. Growing up is a foreign country; you leave home in that sense. The place those children go to, the reason that Vienna in *The Hotel New Hampshire* is as dark as it is and *that* hotel is as dark as it is—and it certainly is the darkest use I've made of Vienna, I think, so far—is that that kind of foreign country is where you go when you're a kid and you lose your mother and one of your siblings or something—that's all just a metaphor for that. And I attempt in the writing, I think, to use the experience of someone else's history, another country's history even, to make somebody painfully aware of his own meager grip on his or her surroundings. The young Garp goes to Vienna to become a writer, but what happens to him is he goes to someplace to realize what it is he wants, that is, he wants to be married and love someone. He goes somewhere to notice that the pursuit of sex without love is a kind of specter that is riddled with death, and it will be later—the whole vagueness of lust will confront him, and its connection with death, be it that baby-sitter later, or be it the results of Helen's affair with Michael Milton. Now, this, I suppose, could be construed as a kind of New England puritanism, but what I see happening to my characters, and what I felt very strongly happen to me, is that the European experience—again, it could have been the Tokyo experience, or I could have gone to Alaska, and I think Alaska would have become a kind of Vienna for me—I just needed to be someplace that removed me from looking with complacency at all the trivia of my surroundings—suddenly it made things not trivial anymore.

GM: But the European experience in your fiction, except in *The Hotel New Hampshire,* is always that of World War II and its aftermath, which was not really *your* experience, and you concentrate very much on the *Anschluss*—in *Setting Free the Bears* you use the *Anschluss* and the Yugoslavian civil war as kind of parallel symbols—the *Anschluss* is always popping up in your writing, and the aftermath of the Yugoslavian civil war comes up again in *The 158-Pound Marriage*. What do these two things mean to you as parallel symbols?

JI: The idea of occupation, principally. I think a part of what I'm doing there, in the case of *Setting Free the Bears* clearly, and in the time that I'm writing about, at least the age of the characters that I'm writing about at that time, in *The 158-Pound Marriage*, I'm saying that . . . well, I grew up in a time, as Siggy says, in *Setting Free the Bears*, when you feel yourself to be sort of taking up the slack in history, . . . you more and more discover that the way you are and the way the world is, is the result of some tremendous upheaval that is in the past, that is, of your parents' generation, and you can sense, with growing eagerness, anticipation, anxiety, that some other kind of confrontation is coming—not strictly politically, or in terms of war. I think that my generation grew up feeling we knew more about World War II than we did about Korea. Korea was small stuff—not for those who were involved in it, not for those whose lives were changed by it—but for someone of my generation growing up, World War II made my parents come out the way they came out, and it made many of the institutions that I would go to and my parents would believe in *the way they were*. Korea was something that happened to somebody's older brother—it wasn't in the same league, so that one tended to know more, fantasize more about, imagine more about this other big thing that one could not have taken part in. *And* one felt that one was in a kind of preparing ground for some clear confrontation with the Communist world, in the form of the limited war that Vietnam was, or in the form of some ultimate nuclear disaster. And I don't think I'm special in my generation in thinking that there was this great thing that you can do nothing about because it's happened and there is this great thing in progress, coming, coming, that you can do nothing about because there's only one of you and it's a large force.

And I suppose I used this representationally or symbolically to underline what seems to me to be the essential feeling of *helplessness* that is your feelings as a teenager, that *is* adolescence—it is that ambiguous period when you are old enough to get pregnant or get somebody else pregnant, but not old enough to pay your taxes or do any of the other things that grown-ups are expected to do. You have a grown-up's body, you have a grown-up's emotional and psychological needs, and you don't have any facility—you don't have the mental equipment, the social equipment. And things like World War II or the ominousness of what might be ahead of us are just overwhelming to you.

GM: Is the great thing that's coming hinted at in *The Hotel New Hampshire* where you play around with *fin de siècle* Vienna—do you see parallels between that and what's happening in America now?

JI: Oh, absolutely. Basically what I did, was I took those kids on a tour of what to me is Old World and New World decadence. I can think of no greater form of old decadence than prostitution—noble, old decadence. Certainly an established form of decadence: I read in the *Times* yesterday that the city is up in arms because prostitutes are taking it to their customers in doorways, and out in the streets, and breaking into parked cars simply to use them as toilets—it's like saying it's alright that we have rats when they're in basements, but now they're coming up above ground and they're coming into the restaurants and something's got to be *done*. There's this sense of prostitution like semen spilling over the city in some way. The whole district attitude, of categorizing it, of the flesh trade—it interested me in *Garp* and

I think I've got a sharper fix on it in *The Hotel New Hampshire*. It's an Old World kind of decadence, and to me, the great New World form, the great contemporary form of it, is the willfulness of terrorism—the belief in an idea to the extent that human beings caught outside or on the other side of that idea are simply expendable—it's the ultimate triumph of a kind of sophomoric Marxism, something that is fascistic in method but vaguely mystical in justification.

GM: I was thinking more about some of the specific political implications—the rise of anti-Semitism, Christian socialism, everything that brought about the rise of Hitler—do you see those kinds of dangers ahead? I just wondered if you had switched your historical focus for some specific reason.

JI: I think you're right; I think politics is threatening, is coming to a head again. The left and right seem to think that there are differences worth spilling blood for again. And I think the social conservatism of this country and the need for some kind of radical change in our domestic policy—though instead of getting a radical change, we're getting a regression back to those sweeter days when the kids didn't fuck until they were nineteen. Well, it's clear what everybody wants: what everybody wants is for the president to bring up their children. Parents can't control their kids anymore. I don't think the gulf between how the parental generation lived and the values they had and the values that young people today have—I don't think that gulf has ever been wider, in this country. And a precedent, of course, for where it was wide, was Nazi Germany in the thirties, when the kids were, many of them, violent Bolsheviks and many more of them brown shirts, who *ratted* on their own parents' loyalty to the right. I don't think the kid in this country feels that he's had representation in the government since Kennedy died—it's the last time kids were interested in politics, in any kind of felt way. And it seems to me that this conservatism that's happening in this country has not so much to do with political conservatism as moral conservatism. You know, Teddy Kennedy isn't being blamed because somebody *died* in his car, but because he was *fucking* somebody—it wouldn't have mattered if he had failed to rescue anybody, but the fact was, he was screwing some young girl, and we've always had strange morality about that. And the flagellants are out, the people who want to return us to pillories—well, it's my part of the country's heritage, isn't it? We're coming on a time when we could crucify our Hester Prynnes again—we're ready to slap the A on the chest of somebody anytime. . . .

GM: Do you see that tied in with all the narcissism in the society?

JI: Sure, I do—everything seems to be some kind of overreaction to everything else. I think the early days of rock and roll were a liberating experience, and the form that it has taken, the—I think—genuinely sadomasochistic forms that it has taken to punk, etc., has been openly hostile toward old people, as if there was this thing that was good, and new, and expressive, and it gave young people something to feel was their own, and the more caviling, *bitchy* members of the old community tried to take it away from them. And that kind of mean-spiritedness engendered other mean-spiritedness, and now it's a *young* mean-spiritedness, where there's a whole group of young people now who really want to *gross out,* as they would say it in their own vernacular, as many people of the so-called conservative generation as possible. This is an open hostility—it's like the polarization between the sexes: like men marching against women and women marching against men. And I've always been interested in that, too; sexual politics has been interesting to me since *The Water-Method Man*—I was too young to know anything about it in *Setting Free the Bears*, but I got interested in the politics of marriage or the politics of separation or the politics of men who want one thing from women and women who want another altogether from men. *This* book *[The Hotel New Hampshire]* is really less political than it is dealing with, making a metaphor, really, of a single sexual act of violence, a *single* sexual trauma—the rape of my hero . . . and if Franny was to be a proper force for me, a proper hero, I wanted to give her two of the most horrible things to overcome I could imagine—one extremely violent and one extremely delicate—the violence being the obvious rape, that betrayal, and the delicate part being that her brother is in love with her.

GM: Since you mention that point—as I read the novel, John seems to be the hero. Why do you consider Franny the hero of the novel?

JI: Well, she's the force one looks up to, I think. Would you consider Nick Carraway the hero of *Gatsby*?—I don't think so, you see, although, in a way, he's the voice that informs the action. Gatsby doesn't know half of what he's doing or why he's going on; he, nonetheless, is the prime mover. And I see Franny, really, as the prime mover.

GM: But she's not the prime grower—she doesn't grow as much as John does. . . .

JI: No, this is true, but then the question is what you want to call someone a hero for—Franny has the most to overcome, and the most to, as Susie the bear would say, *deal* with, and she deals with it. It's not so much a matter of *growth*, as she's almost like a cowboy hero who gets her toes shot off and is dragged behind a horse in the opening of the film, and the rest of the film shows how she puts herself back together again—comes back to the town and cleans up the bad guys.

GM: Do you really think that she puts herself back together again?

JI: No; no more so than I think one really gets satisfying revenge in this world. That whole opera of revenge that they act out on Chipper Dove is, of course, or should be, ultimately, very disappointing— anything short of killing the sonofabitch is going to be a letdown, which they realize. Finally they realize that this should be documented, I think I say, in any proper study of revenge, that to have done something measured, truly in kind, would be to have done too much. And they couldn't have asked for a better script, they couldn't have had a better sting to put on, but ultimately all they do is get the guy to piss in his pants, and it's a big letdown. But, psychologically, what I'm saying is that you maybe never come to terms with such things or deal with such things, though in another way you have to. No more do I think John is truly out of love with Franny—by the end of the book, in fact, he confesses not to be, but he's come close enough to know what it would be like to accept that he couldn't have it. That's the best one can have.

GM: It seems to me the ultimate act of heroism in your novels is to be a good father and a good family man, a committed family man—and that's what John becomes, and what Franny does *not* become: she gives away her child and pursues a career at the expense of family, which your heroes generally come to understand they should not do.

JI: That's a good point—maybe this is a hard novel really to identify a hero in. The dreamer who causes all the action, of course, is the father, but he's hardly a hero . . . though, as Lilly says, "You're all heroes to me"—and I try in the second half of the

book to give everybody their moment. Frank, for
example, could be called a hero in that he has the
farthest to come: he's a thoroughly unlikeable child,
and he becomes almost lofty in his managerial sense
when he's sort of looking out for everybody. He
ultimately becomes that kind of kid who grows on
you—ultimately he really *comes through*. The point, I
guess, is that maybe it's the whole family that is the
hero, because at times none of them could have made
it without help—at times they all need help, take help.
In the end they help the father, but then there's a
moment when the father, as inept and as much of a
dreamer as he is, is actually capable of helping them,
when he gives these marvelous pieces of advice in the
Sacher bar, about things he knows nothing about—it's
still the best advice that anybody could give you, the
most philosophically true. And Lilly bails them out,
more than once, though there's no one, finally, who
can bail her out. Frank, in keeping the books, saves
them all, I suppose because none of them is capable
of that. And the narrator is kind of goody-goody, the
most timid among them, the least expressed, in a
sense. To me, he's a very conventional American
narrator, a Nick Carraway type—that is, someone
who's writing about all the other people in the novel
as if, at least to him, they're all more interesting than
he is. To us, that may not be so; I *like* Nick Carraway.
Ultimately, of course he seems the smartest one of
them all, but he's also the least known, a shadowy
kind of a figure—when he says, "One thing about me:
I always tell the truth," you know pretty well you
better not trust him. And later in the book we find
that Jordan Baker leaves him because he's lied to her.
First-person narrators are always pretending not to
be the hero of their books while always sort of secretly
seeking our sympathy; if they seek it unsecretly, we'll
never give it, so they have to pretend not to want it, I

suppose. So, I guess, in a sense, it's fair to say that the first-person narrator is always the hero of his or her book. . . .

GM: Not in the case of *The 158-pound Marriage,* though.

JI: Quite true. Well, there's a very definite literary first-person narrator—and my only really, in my opinion, literary book, by which I mean it's a book that comes directly out of other books, almost as argument, almost as intellectual debate with two other books which, although I admire them both, both *irritated* me. I said, well, there's another way to see this kind of thing, and it's not the way that either Hawkes's narrator or Ford's narrator sees it. And it seemed to me I wanted to tell a tale by a villain—or as close to a villain as I wanted him to be in that situation—I wanted the person to tell a tale of sexual intrigue, and it seemed to me, that person should most appropriately be the least reliable, the one you can trust the least.

GM: He seems untrustworthy partly because of the way he fits into your own literary values: he's a historical novelist, not an imaginative novelist, and you seem to distrust people who rely too much on history and not enough on imagination—he seems, by your standards, to be someone who has failed not only as a novelist, but also as a human being.

JI: That's very true. He's someone, isn't he, who has great dubiousness for instinct, including the very considerable instinct of his own wife, who Severin Winter recognizes is a peasant—she feels with her feet and thinks with her hands and is, in that sense, a hero to *him,* frustrated and incomplete sort of jock that he is.

GM: You are a writer who generally tries to affirm the human species, and that's your only novel that seems to have a very stark ending. In one

interview you said you were just going through a
pretty morbid frame of mind because none of your
books were selling, so you decided to write a nasty
book—is that the only reason you decided. . . .

JI: Well, I hope I didn't say that I was in a morbid
frame of mind *because* none of my books were selling
—I think what I should have said was that I was in a
morbid frame of mind *and* none of my books were
selling. I was very surprised that *The Water-Method
Man* didn't sell like *hot cakes,* to be perfectly frank. I
didn't write it *to* sell like hot cakes, but of all the books
I've written, including *The Hotel New Hampshire,* as I
look back on them now, the one that I thought was
going to be a bestseller, and still think should have
been, is *The Water-Method Man.* The *most* likely
candidate—I thought a much more likely candidate
for being widely read and enjoyed than *Garp*—it's a
more enjoyable book. It's the only one with a so-to-
speak happy ending.

GM: You mentioned that in that same interview
—I think it was the interview in *Rolling Stone* two
years ago—that you thought that was the only book
that had a happy ending. To me it seems that *all* your
books, except *The 158-Pound Marriage,* have happy
endings . . . affirmative endings, anyway. . . .

JI: That's a better way to say it. Yes, I agree, it is
an affirmative ending. . . .

GM: Why do you say, then, that that book has a
happier ending than *Garp*? . . . *The Hotel New Hampshire* has what seems to me an almost transcendent
ending.

JI: I'm very glad you think so; I would like to
speak of it that way, too—I hope the ending of *The
Hotel New Hampshire* is more spiritually uplifted than
any of the books so far. And yet I think it's also one of
the saddest—that is, the losses that are suffered are
indeed losses.

GM: Is it because nobody dies in *The Water-Method Man?*

JI: That's quite the simplest way of putting it. It's because *The Water-Method Man* is not a book that in its disposition can embrace the kind of violence the other books necessarily do.

GM: But you seem not to be able to get away from it, because your Akthelt and Gunnel subplot has all the violence. . . .

JI: Absolutely. That was once, you know, almost a book by itself. I became so excited when I was doing that part of the book that I realized there was a part of me that found the *mildness* of *The Water-Method Man,* the mainstream story, almost insipid by comparison. I became much more interested, once I had Trumper inventing his thesis, in the Old Norse saga than I was in the book, and the thing threatened to just run away with the novel—I finally just thought, oh hell, I'll just be in service to this muse for a while and follow it and I'll write a book called *Akthelt and Gunnel.*

And I might actually have been saved from that speculation by a Walker Percy book which I've never read, called *Love Among the Ruins.* At the time I laid aside *The Water-Method Man* and I began really in detail doing an Akthelt and Gunnel, which was now called *Love Among the Greths,* and it was to be from Tristan and Isolde to Siegfried to the Icelandic epics —the whole thing was going to be a parody of this kind of bloodshed, a kind of repetition, a wheel, and the principal hero, who would herself be finally slain, would be the woman, Gunnel, who conspires to do in her people with eels. I was having a great time with it, and then this Walker Percy book came out, called *Love Among the Ruins,* and I was so depressed at the idea that I had to think of another title for this thing that it threw me off for about a week or ten days, and

I went back and looked at the pages I had of *The Water-Method Man*. Then I had the feeling I had been trying to make too much of what was a very limited genre, and I felt grateful that I was spared going off on a tangent that I might have been able to call a book of its own—and I think it has, finally, just the right place in *The Water-Method Man*, which is not too big for it. You often have to be lucky to have your perspective saved, I think, and you need something to happen to you to cause you to doubt yourself every so often so you can reassess what it is you're doing and what the priorities are. I got a break in that case. Compared to the blood-shed of Akthelt and Gunnel, I found the rest of *The Water-Method Man* too tame, not enough about life, it seemed to me, or only about the domestic comedy sides of life, and I lost heart in it for a while and then I got it back because it seemed it was alright to write a simply tender, I mean simply affectionate book.

And Bogus Trumper wasn't enough of a character . . . he was a character without sufficient violence—he didn't merit much more of an ending than I was able to give him, whereas in each of the other books, the potential for serious violence was present in the characters. Which is why, despite the sweetness of the narrator's disposition in *The Hotel New Hampshire*, I knew I had to do something to *combat* that disposition, of a purely physical kind, and the whole reason I wanted him to be a weight lifter is that I wanted you to know that he *could* kill some-body, squeezing him to death, and that there was always that potential hanging over what might be-come of Chipper Dove, and something to lend atten-tion, too, to the magnetic quality of his attraction to Franny.

GM: Speaking of *The Hotel New Hampshire*, which

I read as a fairy tale, strict fairy tale—how would you define a fairy tale?

JI: Well, I guess I'm most pleased with *The Hotel New Hampshire* of the five books so far, in that, when I say it's the most fairy tale to me and I'm therefore the most pleased with it, what I mean is that it seems to me the most complete unto itself—that is, it is the most of itself an entered and then left world. You enter it and you get out of it, and while you're in it, *its* rules apply, yours don't. To break that down a little, and say it's also the novel of mine that seems to me requires the least amount of understanding of the so-called *real* and outside world—it is, in that sense, the most completely. . . .

GM: It's your most hermetic novel.

JI: Yes . . . that is, what you have to understand are what the rules of the Hotel New Hampshire are, what the rules of the Berry family are, how *they* operate. It is the most like a *hymn*—fairy tales, of course, always have refrains, these little litanic devices, and I'm getting better at those. I had a few of them going for me in *Garp:* in the world according to Garp, da-da-da-da, we are all terminal cases; we are obliged to remember everything, etc.; the whole Under Toad echo later in the book. But here I got on to the ideas of my refrains—you've got to get obsessed and stay obsessed; you have to keep passing the open windows; Sorrow floats; love, too; doom—those things, like little litanies, little choruses in a simple hymn—I wanted, as in a story for children, to sort of layer them in from an earlier point in time. *And,* I think it is more fairy tale in that it is a book that takes me the furthest away from social realism, which I've never had much fondness for, but in the case of *The World According to Garp,* it was necessary that I commit myself to a fair amount of it—more than I would choose. *Garp* is a novel that has more social realism in

it than the novels I generally choose to read. It *is*
about a writer in a society, it *is* about that society,
those Ellen Jamesians, those people who misunderstand this mother and son alike, or misunderstand
them in different ways. It is probably the most sociological novel I have written and will write. Of a
writer's work, it is the fairy-tale quality of their work
that I enjoy . . . I mean, I love *Anna Karenina* more
than *War and Peace*, I love *First Love* more than *The
Hunting Sketches* or *Fathers and Sons*. . . .

GM: So you see the fairy tale as a certain quality
in writing and not as a strictly definable thing?

JI: Not as a strictly definable thing. I think you
could see, for example, that *The Hotel New Hampshire*
comes most directly, out of anything in my writing,
most directly out of "The Pension Grillparzer" part of
*Garp;* it was while writing that part of *Garp* that I got
the idea for *The Hotel New Hampshire,* the idea of a
novel where there would be this voice, this first-
person voice speaking of various members of his
family, all of them, to him, more interesting than he
is, and using the world of hotels, this sort of transient,
not-quite-real world—because *real* people don't ever
really *live* in hotels—they're supposed to be things
you need, but they're not supposed to be places you
live—if you live in a hotel, you must be in some way a
step out of sync with the rest of the world. And I
developed this idea where I wanted the family in the
hotel business, but *really* in it, not like the judgers of
the hotel business, which the family in "The Pension
Grillparzer" are. I wanted to go through a series of
hotels, each one progressively less of a real hotel and
more of something else.

GM: They each represent a state of mind.

JI: Absolutely. And it's a fairy tale, then, to me,
too, because it's operating most wholly on a symbolic
level. In the beginning of the book, for example,

there is a *real* bear, a *real* rape, a *real* dream—the father's desire to have a perfect hotel—and a little mischief: at the beginning, Freud is just up to mischief, that there is an animal trainer and he's called Freud—but ultimately, this is a book that very symbolically uses hotel, rape, dream, bears. The second bear is no real bear, it's the bear in us, or something. And that rape-crisis center and only successful Hotel New Hampshire is a sort of symbolic manifestation of where you have to live to get over your hurts, where you end up to get over these things. And the dark hotel, which we've talked about, is that phase somewhere between childhood and getting to be a grown-up, that sort of nightmare time you have to go through, where you meet the demons in the world and either come out on top or run away or deal with them however you can. It seemed to me that the world of hotels was perfectly transient, was the perfect opportunity to pick up and go on—*that's* also very fairy tale, that they move a lot, they say, well, so that's it for that hotel and move on.

GM: For Freud, of course, the hotel is a symbol for retreating into a kind of womblike environment—the first and third hotels are very much like that.

JI: Someone asked me recently—he didn't understand why Freud was so *happy* when he realized that he had been chosen to drive the bomb. It's in some sort of a way hidden, but I'd been having mostly fun with Freud and not seriousness with him, but I felt that it was my understanding of the *delight,* finally, in the European Jew, whose people have gone with such appalling little fuss to their death—the *delight* he takes in thinking that he can actually take somebody with him. He's almost like the contemporary Israeli: he's been given an opportunity to *die* in a combative way, which I remember being so struck by when I spent some time in Israel—the feeling so strongly, not simply among young Israelis, but among Israelis of my age and older, that whatever happened to them in Israel, whatever came as a result of the terrible strife in that state—for sure we may all be killed, but we're *never* gonna be killed *that way* again. I think that has enormous psychological importance—that's why, then, Freud said. *"Me? I'm* gonna drive the car? . . . *oh, boy!"*

GM: The real Freud, or "the other Freud," as the children call him is a kind of psychological gloss on the novel, especially in connection with this fairy-tale motif. He's also very present in all your novels, in your preoccupation with the relationship we were talking about earlier, of love and death. . . .

JI: I'm a great fan of Freud.

GM: Well, he seems to be out of favor, now—do you part company with him on a lot of things?

JI: I don't part company with him at all. I'm very old-fashioned and only modestly educated, and I also have grudges that are more personal than intellectual. For example, I know that it's more intelligent to like Jung—at least my more intelligent friends tell me that it's a mark of my only elementary education that I should be so fond of Freud and so lacking in sympathy for Jung, but I remember just a couple of things about Jung, and the thing that prejudices me against him is how *badly* he treated Freud. I think there's something churlish about that, something small-minded about that. Whatever conclusions he came to, he should have stuck up for Freud better than he did—they all should have. And I find it ironic now, that here is a field that has become so *inflated,* so self-important, that really owes itself to a man who was hardly at all interested in himself, and was a real sufferer and a pioneer in a place where he was *most* unwanted. And it seems to me that psychiatrists are a terribly privileged group of people today, and of course what they lack that Freud had in such *abundance* is originality. Freud was a real guesser, and in that sense I take him as, as D. H. Lawrence called him, another kind of novelist.

GM: It's interesting, in connection with Freud, that in a novel that appeared about six months ago, *The White Hotel,* which also uses hotels as you use them, Freud makes his appearance, there's the Holocaust, there's Vienna. . . .

JI: Yes. I hope that each of us is the beneficiary of each other's own, I think, good books—and I do think that's a good book. You know, I hope Mr. Thomas isn't nervous about the fact that there are going to be these two *Hotel* novels out there, and one of them's going to be a piece of shit and one of them's going to be a good book. . . . When I first heard there was going to be a novel called *The White Hotel* and that Freud was a character in it, I was terribly anxious that it was going to be an absolutely rotten book and there would be this kind of confusion, this semantic confusion. I was so delighted, finally, that it was a good book, because then it seems to me that it's a confusion that might benefit both of us. It *is* a good book, too, though so different from mine. His publisher sent it to me before it was published, and she had read my book before it was published, and she said, my gosh, I've read two novels this year that deal with Freud and they're so different—I think you'd enjoy this one.

GM: Thomas indicated that his Freud would probably have been baffled by the Holocaust, while your Freud seems to delight in triumphing over death and over the Holocaust. Your Freud says to the children when he's pointing out the Jewish section and all the empty houses, that "I beat Herr *Tod*"—I triumphed over death—which seems again to reflect the kind of comic vision we were talking about before.

JI: Which, of course, he never does. There's a whole other irony I think one should see in the character of Freud in this book: here's a man who leaves Europe at the right time, he escapes to the United States, he gets out in '33, and he gets fired in Maine, or leaves because he knows he's going to be, by an *anti-Semite,* which drives him back to the continent of the Holocaust, which he survives, only, in a way, to suffer the contemporary Nazi, if you will—this is the way I see the terrorist, as the contemporary fascist spirit, a kind of born-again Nazism—this incredible self-importance, this incredible self-righteousness . . . to *educate,* to *correct.* . . .

GM: Getting back to that, there is a kind of narcissistic tendency in fiction which you're always satirizing—that kind of reflexive, very academic novel. You target that again in *The Hotel New Hampshire,* which is just about the only part of the novel which I really quarrel with, because I didn't think social satire had any place in a fairy-tale novel—it seemed to sort of *intrude* into that kind of universe. . . .

JI: Where does this happen?

GM: At the aftermath of Lilly's suicide. . . . But that aside, you do satirize it in *Garp* and in *The 158-Pound Marriage.* Since you were a professor yourself once, do you think that's all a part of a trend today of too many writers being professors? It used to be, in America anyway, that the novelist came out of the world, so to speak—they were newspapermen—but now, many of the novelists getting "press" are professors, in a sense almost regular professors. Do you think there's a bad connection between these two fields of endeavor?

JI: No, I don't think that's fair—you couldn't blame an institution that has begun to support several marvelous practitioners of the novel for the fact that the novel has many not so marvelous practitioners. I think that the university's interest in the writer, economically that is, in supporting the writer, which is a relatively new thing, is an altogether healthy thing—it's healthy for the university and it certainly has been healthy for the writing community as well. I'm very glad that novelists are not coming to us so exclusively from newspapers and from being journalists. As you know, probably, from other things I've said, I think the autobiographical inclination is one of the least fruitful sources for fiction, or one of the most *abused*. And nothing is served by having the novel remain in the territory of largely hastily educated people. As I get older, I'm less and less impressed with Hemingway; I certainly think that the kind of *bullying* of academia that writers like Nelson Algren used to find fashionable is pretty ridiculous in the light of the fact that some of the country's best writers now *are* academics—and I'm not going to say that their writing is academic. We would never make the assumption that someone who didn't go to school or was not *of* schools, who didn't grow up in an academic community, necessarily had to speak and think like a thug—all you have to do is read somebody like Cheever, who never graduated from prep school— he's one of the most erudite speakers of English prose in this country. . . .

GM: But not a writer who has taught very much in the academic community.

JI: Well, now, once again, you see, the writers who have taught in the academic community—that represents something else again. I'm grateful to the university, really—that it supports a great many good writers—but also it seems to me that the university or the academic community in general represents a very *narrow* view of literature. It's really unfortunate, but we shouldn't blame so much the fact that writers teach now for a living or that universities support them for that, as we should, in general, realize that specialization is killing a lot of things—you know, the designated hitter in baseball is a relatively new phenomenon, too. What I'm saying is: when I was going to school, I was largely brought up on the novels of the nineteenth century, and usually by that I mean the European nineteenth century, because I went to a sort of old-fashioned school that thought that the English novel and the Russian novel were vastly superior to the American novel, and I still think so, in the nineteenth century at least. My father was a Russian historian, and my view of an intellectual, as my father *was*—I am *not*—was someone who had the broadest possible intelligence, which is to say, he had a capacity for understanding *and for enjoying* a wide number of things. He didn't just like one thing: that was the antithesis of intellectual—that was the definition of a garbage man. An intellectual was someone who liked a great number of things because he had an understanding of a great number of things. That seemed obvious to me—it seemed obvious when I read Tolstoy that that was true, and when I read Turgenev that that was true; it seemed obvious to me when I read Hardy that that was true—that *that* was what was to be appreciated there. But I look now at many of the so-called literary journals or literary magazines of my time, and listen to many of the literary arguments of my time, which almost always pit certain kinds of writers against other kinds of writers, and it's very hard to imagine a literary magazine in this country today, not to mention a mainstream magazine, that could, in its narrow aesthetic, publish *both* Virginia Woolf and Thomas Hardy in the same issue; chances are, if they liked one, they couldn't stand the other. This seems to me a *failure* of the intellect, not a triumph of the intellect.

This seems to me to be largely an antiintellectual position, to say that the only writers worth diddly-squat are those people who are writing sentences in such an immaculate and pristine fashion that of course they're no longer interested in narrative or character, blah-blah-blah. . . .

GM: What the professor in *Garp* calls the "new fiction"?

JI: The "new fiction"—right. Well, I can read much of William Gass with interest and pleasure; I also can read John Gardner with interest. I think that only an antiintellectual could truly enjoy settling the argument between them. An intellectual *must* be of the opinion that our literary culture is better for having them both around in it—Gardner for his sloppiness, and Gass for his frequent and considerable lack of substance. And I'm happy to have them both—I mean, one of them does some things beautifully, and somebody else does something else beautifully. What I resent, I think, are the poseurs, who out of their own insecurity for what *they* do seem to find it essential to say "this is what a novel should be," or "this is what a short story should be," or "this is what a writer is," and "this is trash, this is shit, this is bad"—*this* isn't an intellectual position; this is a graduate-student position.

We all know that one of the blights that hits graduate students—it's usually the second-year graduate students, whom I remember the most from teaching—is that it suddenly occurs to them that Djuna Barnes's *Nightwood* is a better book than Joyce's *Dubliners*. The reason for this occurrence is clear—that they needed to *be* second-year graduate students in order to read with much comprehension Djuna Barnes's *Nightwood*, and they realize that *anybody* can read *Dubliners*. Therefore, they're driven to suggest that *Finnegans Wake* is the best thing Joyce ever did, because it takes the greatest amount of scrupulousness and help and attention and other knowledge in order to read it. Well, I think when you get a little older, then, you begin to realize that those books that truly *are* best are those books that speak with some breadth—that it is, for example, an essentially *easy* thing to do to be understood by one's friends, to write a book that only one's friends understand—that this is not a triumph of intellect. We must not confuse the intellect with a desire for elitism. Elitism, it seems to me, is *not* an intellectual position—it's a snobbism, it has nothing to do with an intellectual position.

GM: So Milton's "fit audience, though few" is not for you? That's an elitist position?

JI: I think so. Or, turn that around and say this: I have a good, broad education, and I never went past a couple of years of graduate school—and as anyone knows, an M.F.A. program isn't graduate school, it's fucking around, unless you're using the time well to do your own work, which I did—I didn't read anything in graduate school, I didn't learn anything, I worked on my own work—so I didn't go to graduate school, really; my education was over as an undergraduate. And because I went to a very good prep school, my formal education was virtually over when I left prep school. I'm well read, I read a lot, but I read it my own—that is, without instruction—and I'm very myopic about what I read. I'm very well read in the eighteenth and nineteenth centuries, and I know a whole lot of things in the twentieth century. I don't read much philosophy, I read very little politics. I read a lot of novels, a lot of poetry, and I *hope* that the American novel does not suffer what has happened to the American poem. What I mean by that is very simple: with a modest education—never, for example, a formal course in the seventeenth century, and never a course on Milton, but only so much Milton as one gets in prep school, or only so much Milton as one gets in a sophomore introductory survey to Brit lit—I can read with eighty percent comprehension everything Milton wrote, although his is not my language and his is not my century. I can read with forty percent comprehension at best the poems of my contemporaries, who presume to speak my language and who live in my time, and yet I'm supposed to believe that it is *my* failure that I have trouble with them. I do not appreciate Susan Sontag's fiction; I don't know whom she's writing for—friends, I think, dinner-party conversation. This *can't* be construed as a higher form of intellectual communication, because it's *less* communicative—it simply is. I'm not speaking about popular audiences—of course we know the old argument that if you took *The Sound of Music* and showed it to five hundred people and you took the best of Ingmar Bergman and showed it to five hundred people, unfortunately more of the people would still like *The Sound of Music*—but to people with a minimal education, you know, Bergman is also comprehensible. There's a terrible self-serving, self-congratulatory tone that creeps into that kind of fiction that insists on itself as being "fit for a few."

GM: Is that why you like Donald Justice's poems, because they're accessible?

JI: I'm a *big* fan of Donald Justice's work—I think it has a demanding formality about it, but it has a lucidity about it that's admirable. Anyone who's really tried to write strenuously knows that it's *much* more difficult to be clear than it is to be hard to understand; *anybody* can be hard to understand.

GM: A point is made in this Sunday's *Times,* in a

review of a new Joyce Carol Oates novel, that despite the fact that many critics complain about her cranking out a new novel every year, she is doing what nineteenth-century writers did in creating a *really* gigantic universe—a universe that people do recognize. And isn't that, after all, the function of a novelist?

JI: Well, it is . . . I don't want to be so exclusive, though. One of the things that upsets me so much about modern reviewing—whether or not I take that view of Joyce Carol Oates in particular—one of the problems with contemporary reviewing is that it seems now almost impossible to praise someone without using that praise as a form of gratuitously slurring someone else, so that, somehow, even when they praise you, they manage to put down somebody else. It's very fashionable now, among my intellectual friends, to like Leonard Michaels. Well, I think Leonard Michaels falls into a category of kind of minimalism—it's art that's more intellectualized than it is *realized*. But I wouldn't deny him his position as an artist; I would not say that he is more or less of an artist than I am—he's clearly an artist. He's not possessed of my aesthetic, but I can see that he has one; and if someone in his camp fails to see that I have one, I can only declare that that person is even less of an intellectual than I am, and I'm no intellectual.

GM: Merely having an aesthetic—does that qualify you as an artist?

JI: I think expressing it well does—I mean living it, demonstrating it. Of course, not *having* an aesthetic, but *demonstrating* an aesthetic.

GM: Do you think, then—you seem to hint at it when Freud says in *The Hotel New Hampshire* that "history separates out everything"—do you think literary critics should not try to separate things out, should not eventually create a kind of hierarchy, a judgment that, say, in the twentieth century *this* novelist probably produced the best American writing? Do you think that kind of thing should not take place?

JI: I don't. I don't think that the best and the worst is the way to approach the subject. It makes it sound as if the novel were a form of competition—as if we had rules, as if someone were keeping score. In the long run, of course, readers keep score, and they may not keep the best score in our own lifetime, but maybe in the long run they do.

GM: Eventually doesn't it seem that the critics keep the score? Because the books that get passed on from generation to generation, or the books that one is exposed to in college. . . .

JI: I think this is only true, then, if you're a bad teacher. If you're a good teacher, I know that you can't teach books that don't work more than once. I've tried to force books on students that *just* don't go down. . . .

GM: But you also can't teach books that aren't in print. If you're teaching the nineteenth-century novel, you teach Dickens and Brontë and Thackeray; the novelists of the nineteenth century who may have been popular in their own time but are now inaccessible because you can't get the books—haven't they been "separated out" by a kind of critical process that dictates the choices of the publishing industry?

JI: That's true, I think, though, what I would like to see more of in criticism is the critic coming to terms with the aesthetic of the particular writer and holding the writer responsible for the writer's own universe—holding the writer responsible for living by the rules *he* sets up.

GM: But there still must be a selection: in a thirteen-week course, you can only choose to teach twelve novels—so how do you choose the twelve?

JI: I suppose by variety. It seems to me that *is* the advantage of the novel, ultimately. God help us if we ever go the way of contemporary American *painting,* let's say—you know, have you *been* to the Whitney Bi-annual the last couple of years?—it's appalling. When I go to New York now, this pinnacle of art in this country—and I go to New York a *lot*—I go to the Frick and look at the old Corots and the old Rembrandts, which I've seen a hundred times, but I won't go to a new gallery, I won't go and see a new show, unless I know ahead of time the work of a particular painter whom I like is going to be there. I have *no* confidence whatsoever in what the hell I'm going to see at the Whitney—*none.*

GM: Do you think that's a problem of the media —by which I mean, by now, obviously, publishing has become very tied in as a media event. The publication of *The Hotel New Hampshire* is going to be a real media event—it's already been labeled one of the "big books" that are coming out in the fall. And the critics seem to be getting into the game as well, insofar as the tendency is spreading to label every other novel that comes out as an important book, as perhaps "the great American novel."

JI: Yes, well, you see, the reason they're doing this, they're setting you up—they're like people planting ducks in a shooting gallery: before you can shoot them, you've got to lift their heads above the horizon, and I think that you'll see that very clearly with *The Hotel New Hampshire.* People insisted on the *greatness* of *Garp* the last time, and now that I have been raised above the horizon, people are going to find ways to insist on the disappointment of *The Hotel New Hampshire.* Well, little of this matters to me or the way I

work. I know that by my own aesthetic, I was pleased
with the last half of *Garp*—very pleased with it, and
very pleased with what I got down to in that book.
But I had a shaky time in the early going with it—it
was raggedly put together, and I feel about it a little
like a tailor who sees somebody walking away in a suit
that everybody else says looks like a good suit, but
they can't see the seams, but he remembers how many
times he had to cut the pant-leg, you know what I
mean? You can't see it, I think. I think the patchwork
was pretty well done; I think the editing after the
filming was pretty well snipped and cut and pasted
back together so that you can't see the seams. But *I*
see the seams—I know that the *making* of that book
was not a smooth and satisfying aesthetic event—it
was a long time spent rowing out in this direction, and
a long time spent rowing back, and then rowing out
here and rowing out there and finally getting on the
right track and going back to make all the other boats
look like they'd been going that direction to begin
with. And I think I did a pretty good job of patching
things up, but it's a *patched-up* book. Oddly, only two
of the books, *Setting Free the Bears* and *The Hotel New
Hampshire* were books that remained truthful to their
original conceptions. Now that's just an aesthetic of
mine; it probably doesn't matter to anybody else, but
it's like I'm the tailor, and when I see the well-dressed
man walk away from the office, I'm the only one who
knows how many times I had to put the zipper
in—ultimately you get the zipper right, or you
wouldn't let it go. Well, it means so little, except to
one's economic livelihood, or one's popular reputa-
tion, what the so-called critics say about your work.

GM: Is popular criticism more show-biz than
anything else?

JI: Or, it seems to me, more *absent* than anything
else. I mean, I can't help but feel, since I've had both

shoes on my feet now, that, since I feel I've been largely ignored for books that should have been given *some* attention. . . .

GM: But you did get mostly good reviews—not *prominent* reviews—for the first three books.

JI: Yes, and now I can expect, with irritation in advance, some backbiting about what I think is my best-made book to date—people who aren't going to deal unfairly with *The Hotel New Hampshire,* but people who wish they had had the opportunity to say a few nasty things about *Garp,* or at least about how well it did, and I'm going to have my *bank account* reviewed. So that, if people think—and there are people who do—that you can never take a popular novel seriously—I'll tell you one thing you can't take seriously, and that's what people *write* about popular novels, either the good or the bad. There are always a couple of popular novels that are very good; the majority, of course, are very bad. I always question people to point out to me, though, how this statistic is different than all the novels that are unpopular—eighty percent of the novels that are unpopular are shit, too, and some of them are worse shit, because they presume to be more. Something about a junky best-seller that's awful: at least it's a book without pretensions to art, I read some of the bad books that pretend to be art, too. . . . I mean, it's hard to judge between unlikeable art when one thinks it's all so unlikeable.

But this is a long way from what I started to say about an aesthetic of mine, in viewing the novel, both as something to teach and as a thing to be reviewed—it's the marvelous *breadth* within the form. I'm amazed, for example, at the work of Günter Grass—I mean, here's a living author who, in my opinion, has written the greatest long novel by a living writer, in *The Tin Drum,* and the greatest short novel, in *Cat and*

*Mouse,* and clearly they're books by the same author, but to be able to switch aesthetic gears as well as he did in the case of those two books, to write something that's so succinct and understated and *sly,* and then to write something that is so ribald, robust, and all over the place, so baroque—is a demonstration of a man so *comfortable* with the spaciousness of the form, and I want to see more of that kind of thing appreciated. I *love* the work of John Cheever: I think it has a fussy, neat, everything-in-its-place quality that's sort of like the house of a beloved grandmother—stories populated with *beautiful* objects that all fit, that all work—I don't think there's been a better writer of short stories since Chekhov, and I *hate* the assumption that because a new book comes out every three months and is called the best of this or the worst of that, that we're supposed to not extend some superlatives when they apply.

I think the things that Vonnegut has been doing to the novel over the last ten or fifteen years are admirable for their originality—they're *not* all successful. By his own admission, I think he's capable of writing first-rate books and kind of B novels, and you never know what you're going to get, but even a B novel by Vonnegut is an original piece of work, and it's a work that *tests* the form. I think he's going to come out with a book one day that's going to be 399 pages of introduction and then a two-page novel. You see what I'm saying: how much literature would be shrunk if we had to choose between John Hawkes and Kurt Vonnegut—*think* of the reduction of the pleasures that the novel can give us if we have to say that Barth and Gass and Barthelme are the only people who are doing it right, and everybody else should get off the ship—I don't want *anybody* to get off the ship. I mean, let's be clear that there are people who don't count, like Judith Krantz, but everybody else counts.

GM: I wanted to ask you about your first two stories—one is called "The Winter Branch."

JI: Gee, you probably remember that more than I do. . . . *Redbook* published it, right?

GM: Right. Then there was another one that appeared in the *Boston Review* about someone named Minna, and I can't remember the title. . . .

JI: I borrowed that story from my wife, actually.

GM: But they're so different from your later work—were you consciously trying to imitate somebody else then?

JI: I don't think self-consciously, because I was too young—I was in college when I wrote both of those stories. And I think that the feeling I had with both of them was that they were mainly imitative. . . .

GM: What were you trying to imitate? They both seem like the classic well-made short story.

JI: I think that's a good way to put it. That certainly is true of "A Winter Branch." I was trying to write a very quiet, understated story in which a small thing happens, and the thing that happens is not named, but what happens is visualized by an event, the flight of an animal, a track in the snow. . . .

GM: Hemingway-like?

JI: Yes, a very small object. And then there's a very straightforward piece of sort of social sadness— in the story of the boy and the old woman who work in a kitchen at the college ["Weary Kingdom"]. As you discover in later things, sociology has never become my mainstream, but that's a very sociological little story about what working-class people have to put up with—the brats of the educated class.

GM: What happened to the movie of *Setting Free the Bears*?

JI: It just never got made. It was cast, it was

scripted, an option was renewed, but that's as far as it went. It just went through those stages.

GM: Do you have any more desire to write for the movies?

JI: No, I really don't. I'm interested in the movies, interested in writing a short novel, a novella that could be more easily converted to film.

GM: Does the form come first to you—the desire to write a fairy-tale novel, or a short novel . . . ?

JI: Yes, the form frequently does come first—I very much have a sense of the form of this new book and had very much a sense of the form of this other one, the way it's formed by hotels.

# Notes

## 1. LIFE AND ART

1. Thomas Williams, "Talk with John Irving," *The New York Times Book Review*, 23 April 1978, p. 26.
2. Greil Marcus, "John Irving: The World of 'The World According to Garp'," *Rolling Stone*, 13 December 1979, p. 70.
3. Williams, p. 26.
4. Marcus, p. 70.
5. Marcus, p. 70.
6. Marcus, p. 71.
7. "Irving, John" in Charles Moritz, ed., *Current Biography Yearbook 1979* (New York: The H. W. Wilson Co., 1979), pp. 178–81. I am indebted to this article and to Greil Marcus's piece, cited above, for much of the biographical information in this chapter.
8. Stephen E. Rubin, " 'Garp': Setting Free a Best Seller," *Chicago Tribune Book World*, 11 May 1980, Sec. 7, p. 2.
9. Rubin, p. 2.
10. Marcus, p. 72.
11. Rubin, p. 2.
12. John Irving, "Kurt Vonnegut and His Critics," *The New Republic*, 22 September 1979, pp. 41–42.
13. Irving, "Kurt Vonnegut and His Critics," p. 42.

212

14. Michael Priestly, "An Interview with John Irving," *New England Review* I (1979): 498–99.
15. Priestly, p. 491.
16. John Irving, "In Defense of Sentimentality," *The New York Times Book Review*, 25 November 1979, p. 3.
17. Irving, "In Defense of Sentimentality," p. 96.
18. John Gardner, *On Moral Fiction* (New York: Basic Books, 1978), p. 198.
19. Priestly, p. 498.
20. John Irving, *The Water-Method Man* (1972; rpt. New York: Pocket Books, 1978), pp. 69–70 (Chapter 10).
21. Priestly, p. 500.
22. William Wordsworth, *Selected Poems and Prefaces,* ed. Jack Stillinger (Boston: Houghton Mifflin Co., 1965), pp. 446–47.
23. Terence Des Pres, "Introduction," *3 By Irving* (New York: Random House, 1980), p. xv.

## 2. IN THE VIENNA WOODS

1. "Interview with John Irving," *Options,* WGBH Radio, Boston, August 13, 1979.
2. Gordon Brook-Shepherd, *Anschluss* (London: Macmillan & Co., 1963), p. xiii.
3. Greil Marcus, "John Irving: The World of 'The World According to Garp'," *Rolling Stone,* 13 December 1979, p. 71.
4. Ibid.

## 3. TRUMPER'S COMPLAINT

1. Greil Marcus, "John Irving: The World of 'The World According to Garp'," *Rolling Stone,* 13 December 1979, p. 72.
2. Michael Priestly, "An Interview with John Irving," *New England Review,* I, No. 4 (Summer 1979): 503.
3. George Dickerson, "Review of *The Water-Method Man* by John Irving," *Time,* July 24, 1972, p. 81.

## 4. THE GOOD WRESTLER

1. Greil Marcus, "John Irving: The World of 'The World According to Garp'," *Rolling Stone,* 13 December 1979, p. 72.

2. Ford Madox Ford, *The Good Soldier* (1915; rpt. New York: Vintage, 1955), pp. 18–19.

3. John Kuehl, *John Hawkes and the Craft of Conflict* (New Brunswick: Rutgers University Press, 1975), p. 137.

4. Ibid., p. 149.

5. Martin Esslin, *The Theater of the Absurd* (New York: Anchor Books, 1961), p. 316.

6. John Hawkes, *The Blood Oranges* (New York: New Directions, 1971), p. 35.

7. I am indebted for this idea to Robert Graalman, who taught me a lot about wrestling.

8. Djuna Barnes, *Nightwood* (1937; rpt. New York: New Directions, 1961), p. 121.

9. Louis F. Kannenstine, "Djuna Barnes and 'The Halt Position of the Damned'," in *A Festschrift for Djuna Barnes on Her 80th Birthday,* ed. Alex Gildzen (Kent, Ohio: Kent State University Libraries, 1972).

## 5. PORTRAIT OF THE ARTIST AS A NERVOUS WRECK

1. Terence Des Pres, "Review of THE WORLD ACCORDING TO GARP by John Irving," *The New Republic,* 29 April 1978, p. 32.

2. Marcus Aurelius, *Meditations,* trans. Maxwell Staniforth (New York: Penguin, 1964), p. 51. I have referred to this translation here because it is the one Irving seems to have used. The best edition of the *Meditations,* however, is A. S. L. Farquharson's (London: Oxford University Press, 1944).

3. Aurelius, p. 115.

4. Aurelius, p. 177.

5. Randall Jarrell, "The Death of the Ball Turret Gunner," in *The Complete Poems* (New York: Farrar, Straus & Giroux, 1969), p. 144.

6. Laurence Sterne, *The Life and Opinions of Tristram Shandy, Gentleman* (1759; rpt. Boston: Houghton Mifflin Co., 1965), p. 3.

7. Des Pres, p. 32.

8. Ivar Ivask, Introduction, *The Poor Fiddler* by Franz Grillparzer (New York: Frederick Ungar Publishing Co., 1967), p. 14. This is the same edition that Garp reads in the novel.

9. Aurelius, p. 127.

10. I have used Edith Hamilton's rendering of the myth in *Mythology* (New York: New American Library, pp. 270–71), which is more explicit in detailing the particular nature of the metamorphosis than Ovid.

11. Aurelius, p. 188.

12. Aurelius, p. 159.

13. Greil Marcus, "John Irving: The World of 'The World According to Garp,'" *Rolling Stone,* 13 December 1979, p. 72.

14. Aurelius, p. 60.

## 6. MY FATHER'S ILLUSIONS

1. Bruno Bettelheim, *The Uses of Enchantment* (1976; rpt. New York: Vintage, 1977), p. 25.

2. Bettelheim, p. 45.

3. Bettelheim, p. 45.

4. Michael Priestly, "An Interview with John Irving," *New England Review* I (1979): 491–92.

5. Sigmund Freud, *Civilization and Its Discontents,* trans. and ed. James Strachey (New York: Norton, 1961), p. 38.

6. Joseph Campbell, *The Hero with a Thousand Faces* (1949; rpt. Princeton: Princeton University Press, 1973), p. 30.

7. Bettelheim, p. 105.

8. Bettelheim, p. 106.

9. Bettelheim, p. 117.

10. Bettelheim, p. 40.

11. Campbell, p. 72.

12. Campbell, p. 77.

13. Campbell, p. 79.
14. Bettelheim, p. 100.
15. Freud, *Civilization and Its Discontents,* p. 69.
16. Bettelheim, p. 102.
17. Bettelheim, p. 40.
18. Bettelheim, p. 100.
19. Carl E. Schorske, *Fin-de-Siècle Vienna* (1980; rpt. New York: Vintage, 1981), p. 6.
20. Schorske, p. 6.
21. Schorske, pp. 8–9.
22. Frederic Morton, *A Nervous Splendor* (Boston: Atlantic/ Little Brown, 1979), p. 315.
23. Morton, p. 315.
24. Campbell, p. 193.
25. Bettelheim, p. 79.
26. Sigmund Freud, *The Interpretation of Dreams,* trans. and ed. James Strachey (New York: Avon, 1965), p. 87.
27. Bettelheim, p. 309.
28. Bettelheim, p. 309.
29. Bettelheim, p. 73.

# Bibliography

## 1. BOOKS

*Setting Free the Bears.* New York: Random House, 1968.
*The Water-Method Man.* New York: Random House, 1972.
*The 158-Pound Marriage.* New York: Random House, 1974.
*The World According to Garp.* New York: E. P. Dutton, 1978.
*3 By Irving.* New York: Random House, 1980. (Includes *Setting Free the Bears, The Water-Method Man* and *The 158-Pound Marriage,* with an introduction by Terence Des Pres)
*The Hotel New Hampshire.* New York: E. P. Dutton, 1981.

## 2. SHORT STORIES

(including stories composed independently and later incorporated into *Garp,* but not excerpts from that novel published in *Playboy, Swank, Gallery,* and *Penthouse*)

"A Winter Branch." *Redbook,* November 1965, pp. 56 and 143–46.

"Weary Kingdom." *The Boston Review,* Spring–Summer 1968, pp. 8–35.

"Lost in New York." *Esquire,* March 1973, pp. 117 & 152.

"Almost in Iowa." *Esquire,* November 1973, pp. 144–46 and 224–29.

"Brennbar's Rant." *Playboy,* December 1974, pp. 137 & 304–307.

"Students: These Are Your Teachers!" *Esquire,* September 1975, pp. 68 & 156–59.

"The Pension Grillparzer." *Antaeus,* Winter 1976, pp. 7–27.

"Vigilance." *Ploughshares* 4, 1977, pp. 103–14.

"Dog in the Alley, Child in the Sky," *Esquire,* June 1977, pp. 109 & 158–62.

"Interior Space." *Fiction* 6, 1980, pp. 26–58. (This story was written in 1974.)

## 3. Essays and Non-Fiction

"Gorgeous Dan." *Esquire,* April 1973, pp. 106–9 & 217–21.

"Life After Graduation According to Garp." *Esquire,* March 27, 1979, p. 53.

"Best Seller: What Does it Really Mean?" *Vogue,* April 1979, pp. 154 & 156.

"Kurt Vonnegut and His Critics." *The New Republic,* September 22, 1979, pp. 41–49.

"In Defense of Sentimentality." *The New York Times Book Review,* November 25, 1979, pp. 3 & 96.

"TABA Winners: No Thanks and Thanks." *The New York Times Book Review,* May 25, 1980, pp. 4 & 14–15. (Irving discusses why he was happy to accept his American Book Award; Christopher Lasch writes about why he didn't accept his.)

## 4. Book Reviews (selected)

Elkin, Stanley. *The Living End. The New York Times Book Review,* June 10, 1979, pp. 7 & 30.

Wolff, Geoffrey. *The Duke of Deception. The New York Times Book Review,* August 12, 1979, pp. 1 & 18–19.

Phillips, Jayne Anne. *Black Tickets. The New York Times Book Review,* September 30, 1979, pp. 13 & 28.

Morrison, Toni. *Tar Baby. The New York Times Book Review,* March 29, 1981, pp. 1 & 30–31.

## 5. Miscellaneous

"For Fitch Retired." (a poem) *Year of Dog*. Putney, Vt.: The Year of Dog, 1972.

"Neglected Books of the Twentieth Century." *Antaeus*, Autumn 1977, pp. 131–32. (Irving contributes a list of books he considers neglected.)

"Works in Progress." *The New York Times Book Review*, July 15, 1979, pp. 1 and 14. (Irving discusses *The Hotel New Hampshire*.)

## 6. Interviews

Williams, Thomas. "Talk with John Irving." *The New York Times Book Review*, April 23, 1978, pp. 26–27.

Bannon, Barbara. "PW Interviews John Irving." *Publishers Weekly*, April 24, 1978, pp. 6–7.

de Coppet, Laura. "John Irving." Interview, October, 1981, pp. 42–44.

"His World of Garp is a Place of Black Comedy and Wild Invention: Ah Yeth!" *People*, December 25, 1978.

O'Toole, Lawrence. "John Irving Adjusts: Is There Life After Garp?" *Macleans*, June 11, 1979, pp. 4–6.

Priestly, Michael. "An Interview with John Irving." *New England Review* I (Summer 1979): 489–504.

Marcus, Greil. "John Irving: The World of 'The World According to Garp'." *Rolling Stone*, December 13, 1979, pp. 68–75.

West, Richard. "John Irving's World After 'Garp'." *New York Magazine*, August 17, 1981, pp. 29–32.

Suplee, Curt. "John Irving and the Tyranny of the Imagination," *The Washington Post*, August 25, 1981, Section B, pp. 1 and 8–9.

Sheppard, R. Z. "Life into Art." *Time*, August 31, 1981, pp. 46–51.

# Index

# DATE DUE

| | | | |
|---|---|---|---|
| | | | |
| | | | |
| | | | |
| | | | |
| | | | |
| | | | |
| | | | |
| | | | |
| | | | |
| | | | |
| | | | |
| | | | |
| | | | |
| | | | |
| | | | |
| | | | |

Demco, Inc. 38-293